Myth ar

Myth and Mystery

Who were the first Europeans to visit New Zealand?

John Tasker

TANDEM PRESS

First published in New Zealand in 1997 by
TANDEM PRESS
2 Rugby Road, Birkenhead, North Shore City,
New Zealand

Cover illustration by Paul Woodruffe
Cover design by Ben Archer/Moscow Design
Book design and production by Graeme Leather
Printed and bound by GP Print, Wellington

Contents

Introduction

Were unidentified non-Polynesians present in New Zealand before the arrival of James Cook in 1769? In the pages which follow, a determined attempt has been made to find an answer to this 225-year-old problem. For it was Cook himself who first posed the question when he asked South Island Maori: 'Has a ship such as ours ever been on this coast before?' The answers he received then set a precedent for all who have asked the same question since. Some Maori said no. Others yes. And so it is today. On the one hand most scholars believe a lack of documentation works against the idea, while on the other, supporters of the notion point to circumstantial evidence which in their opinion is so compelling that they question the wisdom of anyone ever wanting to dismiss it.

What this latter group is saying in effect is that New Zealand has two histories. An official one, as taught in our learning institutions. And an unofficial version, charged with so much interest and drama that it deserves to be investigated much more fully than it has been. It all boils down to which non-Polynesian was first to gaze upon the shores of Aotearoa. Tasman? Or somebody else? And was Cook the first European to set foot on our soil?

The idea of a pre-Cook, European presence in this country has been around for a very long time. It hasn't gone away because attached to it is an element of truth so strong that no amount of heavy artillery from the academic community has been able to put a dent in it, so stubborn that it persists with ease from generation to generation, and so deeply rooted that it took on a life of its own right from the very beginning of Maori-European contact. And it continues to cling to this life with a dogged determination.

Many will ask: what does it matter which non-Polynesian first walked on a New Zealand beach? What possible relevance could such an event have for us today? Except to set the record straight, the answer is – probably none. The real value of such an exercise lies more in the new information likely to be uncovered along the way – information of a type which another century or two of neglect may well obscure altogether. When you run a vacuum cleaner across a carpeted floor you don't just pick up dust; other small items go rattling up the pipe as well. And in this book, as we go probing about in the dark little corners of New Zealand's past, we will discover much the same sort of thing and find people whom time seems to have forgotten, events overlooked by historians, and objects whose presence in this country cannot be accounted for in the light of current knowledge.

The subject is long overdue for serious examination, and although the following is an attempt to do just this, the material presented should not be regarded as a dossier of completed research projects. Because it isn't. It would be far more correct to view it as a catalogue of potentially helpful clues and suggestions – or as pieces of information which may one day result in a resolution of our lead question. And nothing more.

Acknowledgements

This book would not have been possible without the input of a great many people. I would like to thank:

Barbara Else of T.F.S. Literary Agency, whose professional guidance made all the difference.

Trevor Hosking, who encouraged me to persist against the odds.

Officers and staff of the Alexander Turnbull Library, Wellington, who over a period of several years responded to my endless enquiries with patience and skill.

Writers past and present who touched on my subject to one degree or other, and from whose works I borrowed: A.G. Bagnall, J.C. Beaglehole, J. Herries-Beattie, A.C. and N.C. Begg, E. Best, J. Buller, R. Duff, W.J. Elvy, B. Fell, R. Hervé, C.G. Hunt, C.W. Ingram and P.O. Wheatley, R. Langdon, S. Lee and T. Kendall, R. McConnell, K.G. McIntyre, R. McNab, A.K. Newman, J.L. Nicholas, T. Ollivier, J. Robertson, A. Salmond, A.S. Thomson, J. White and H.W. Williams.

Officials of various institutions around the world who went out of their way to co-operate. I would particularly like to thank: François Bellec and Annie Madet, Director and Documentalist, Musée de la Marine, Paris; Lt. Colonel de Gislain De Bontin, Chief of Historical Services, Ministry of Defence, France; Jennifer Broomhead, Copyright and Permissions Librarian, State Library of New South Wales, Australia; Judith Cannon, Pictorial Reference Librarian, National Library of Australia; Miss C.M. Hall, Department of Manuscripts, the British Library; A. Harkink, Royal Dutch Geographical Society, Amsterdam; M. Philippe Henrat of the French National Archives;

José Ignacio Gonzalez-Aller Hierro, Spanish Naval Museum, Madrid; Edwin Hofbauer, Austrian National Library; Brian Thynne, Hydrography Section and Liza Verity, Enquiry Services, National Maritime Museum, London; Diedrick Wildeman and Jan van Zijverden, Scheepvaart Museum, Holland; and Eva Yocum, Photographic Information Co-ordinator, Museum of New Zealand, Wellington.

And I have to thank those people and organisations who helped in other ways: Janet Davidson, Daryl Griggs, Des Harris, Noel Hilliam, Nat Mitchell, Christine Mortellier, Nelson Historical Society and Mick Wordsworth.

1

The Contribution of Maori Folklore

The Treasure of Maori History

In looking towards oral Maori tradition for clues of a pre-Cook, European presence in New Zealand we need to be comfortable with the idea that this particular source of information is valid. Because if it isn't, the dozen or so prehistoric ship visits mentioned deserve no further consideration. If it is, then it should be treated with respect because, so far as the movements of people in New Zealand prior to 1769 are concerned, what we have locked up in Maori folklore is all we are ever likely to get.

So can we believe what the stories seem to be saying? Did they begin as factual accounts of past events? Or is the material so nebulous it can be said to have little or no historical value whatever? A recent event in Australia goes a long way towards clarifying our attitude to queries of this nature.

In June 1993, the discovery was reported of a shipwreck of ancient appearance buried in the sands just south of Byron Bay in northern New South Wales. Carbon dating of a wooden peg taken from the wreck placed the age of the find at somewhere between AD 1450 and AD 1660 – up to 320 years before James Cook charted the east coast of Australia. Historian Dr Bill Boyd of New England University said of it in an interview (*TV1 News*, June 1993):

> I think it is an extremely exciting discovery. If the evidence is as good as it is suggesting it might be then we are really on to something here. And it could have implications for New Zealand. If Portuguese or Spanish ships were on the east coast of Australia well before Cook it adds weight to the theory that they were also in New Zealand before Cook – or even Tasman.

This is interesting enough in itself, but there is more. Dr Boyd makes the incident relevant to this chapter by touching on a further implication for New

Zealand. He said that the carbon dating gave credence to a local Aboriginal folktale which spoke of the wreck and its old-time occupants long before the actual discovery was made.

The Australian tradition related how pale-skinned strangers in a large ship had once prowled the New South Wales coast centuries ago, coming ashore in the Byron Bay area to rape local women, and to cart them off as slaves. Eventually the Aboriginal men were able to take control of the ship and to kill off its crew in retaliation. The craft drifted on to the beach and in time was swallowed up by the sands where it has survived intact to the present day – largely, it is thought, because a curse placed on the site by tribal elders has prevented any interference with it over the centuries. The wreck has not yet been dug up and examined thoroughly, but moves are under way to obtain a licence to survey it, and once this is completed an identification can be made, and a positive age ascribed.

This Australian story is almost identical to a number of Maori tales which feature the same sort of thing here. Except that on this side of the Tasman we don't need to rely on the discovery of previously unknown shipwrecks to prove the historical value of our folktales. Especially those which pertain to the last five hundred years or so. There is no doubt that the appearance of independent confirmation in the form of relevant physical evidence would be welcome in some cases, but even without this scholars have conceded for decades that the Maori traditional record can be no less than a factual account of the past – give or take a few minor embellishments.

Sir Maui Pomare was so consumed by this idea, and so afraid that his death would mean the loss of such a large amount of tradition, that he pushed himself to the limit just before he died in a race to get it all down on paper.

Dr Pei Te Hurinui Jones had a lifelong passion for collecting the traditions of the Tainui people and was utterly convinced that the material he amassed was factual history. He died in 1976, and it wasn't until 1995 that this was all published in book form (*Nga Iwi o Tainui*) – a massive 68 chapters of it – in an event which was described in academic circles as 'long awaited'.

Anaru Reedy in 1993 (*Nga Korero o Mohi Ruatapu*) pointed out that ancient Maori history comes in two forms: a 'rich oral tradition', and a written 'taonga'. The latter is composed of a vast amount of largely untranslated and unpublished manuscript material produced by Maori writers in the 19th century. In exhorting all iwi to locate and publish as much of this as they could Reedy said that its importance 'will become increasingly apparent in the years that lie ahead'.

So Maori tradition and lore as a body is now taken very seriously indeed, and rightly described as a 'treasure'. But that part of it which interests us in this book sometimes comes with in-built difficulties; the problem being how to differentiate between centuries-old fact and centuries-old fiction which may have inadvertently become attached to the original truth. This may seem an impossible task so long after the event, but Drs A.C. and N.C. Begg in their book (*Port Preservation*) in 1973 demonstrate how some people have been able to achieve this very thing with various pieces of tradition they have dealt with:

> In some legendary tales it may be difficult to determine which is the hard core of fact and which are embellishments. Yet many of the Maori folk stories have been fully proven. Acting on evidence from a Murihiku legend Dr G. Orbell found the supposedly extinct takahe still living in the district described. Later he followed another Murihiku legend to the greenstone deposits near Lake Wakatipu, or Te Wai Pounamu. Because he believed a legend about a Maori princess buried somewhere along the shores of Lake Hauroko, Mr William Evans spent a lifetime looking for the grave. A generation later his son, Mr George Evans, found the burial place. Legend can never be discounted. As J.V. Luce has pointed out (*End of Atlantis*, London, 1970), classical scholars laughed at Schliemann when he set out with Homer in one hand and a spade in the other. But he dug up Troy, and demonstrated that it is rash indeed to underestimate the historical value of folk memory.

An Angry Sky over the Kaipara

If not rash, then certainly unwise. But so much for past breakthroughs. What's happening in New Zealand today? Is anyone continuing the process of prising historical fact from ancient tradition? The story which follows is the most dramatic attempt yet to prove the veracity of a Maori folktale.

Farmer-historian Noel Hilliam of Dargaville has long been fascinated by the history of the Kaipara harbour and its 4000-kilometre shoreline. He is familiar with most Maori folklore of the region and his interest extends to investigating those portions of it which appear to him to hold out some promise of a resolution. A no-nonsense realist, he does his best to maintain some sort of scepticism and objectivity when it comes to dealing with the historical theories released from folklore, and he is constantly trying to find solid evidence to back those theories.

This problem is approached on several different levels at the same time. For instance, when Hilliam was younger, there were 110 identified shipwrecks in the district. His own historical researches since then have raised that total to 149, and there are other wrecks he is still trying to identify. As a result of countless scuba-diving expeditions the sheds on the family farm soon began to swell with the increasing number of relics brought home each time. So it is not surprising to learn he helped found the Northern Wairoa Maori, Maritime and Historical Museum Society, and was its president for 12 years. The result of the Society's efforts is one of the neatest small museums in the country, on a hilltop site overlooking the Kaipara and dominated by the masts of the *Rainbow Warrior*.

Once up and running, however, Hilliam gave up formal links with the museum in order to concentrate on his principal passion – the unearthing of new historical fact as triggered off by personal discovery, and the decoding of Maori folklore. In 1982 the one led to the other. Called out by Search and Rescue authorities to use his aircraft in the hunt for a missing fisher off Bayly's Beach, he not only sighted the body, but something else which set his pulses racing. Poking up out of the sand close inshore was a D-shaped object which on closer examination turned out to be the outline of a wreck unlike any he had ever seen before. The wreck appeared to be that of a Spanish caravel of the 16th century – broad in the stern and then narrowing to rounded bows. According to an article in the *New Zealand Herald* of 19 May 1990:

> News of that discovery leaked out at the time, with one good result. It brought contact with a botanist named Jim Cox who since the 1950s had been searching the banks of the Northern Wairoa River for a fabled stone

altar. Hilliam says the story was this: In the 1950s Cox had been in hospital alongside an elderly Yugoslav gumdigger. The digger told him that in 1902 he and friends had been engaged to clear kahikatea scrub for farmland along the banks of the river. Among the scrub they found a stone altar, with roots of the trees growing through it.

Hilliam was excited by the idea of trying to locate the altar, so began a search of his own. He tried first by air, looking for the likely spot from above. When that failed, he searched through local district records in the hope that some small clue might emerge which would help him pinpoint it. On a 19th-century survey map, though, he found something which was to prove much more interesting. There was no information on the altar, but he discovered the first clue to the whereabouts of a possible pre-Tasman shipwreck. This was indicated on the map by remnants of a piece of local lore concerning a centuries-old incident of which the surveyor had jotted down only tantalising snippets. It must have been a dramatic event to have survived in lore so long, and a well-known one too, for the surveyor to have picked up on it in the first place and to have written down what he did.

On the map the word 'Rangiriri' was inscribed at a spot near the river, and an adjacent notation on the old document said: 'Where 100 warriors were wiped out in an instant.' According to local Maori lore this apparent disaster was supposed to have been caused by an enormous explosion. But the question is: what sort of an explosion? What had the 100 warriors been exposed to which was capable of causing their death instantly? The disastrous event seems to have occurred long before Cook and Tasman's time. Pre-contact Maori simply didn't have the technology to cause explosions of the kind required. So the explanation – when it came – would have to be a very interesting one. It certainly had Noel Hilliam scratching his head: 'That area [marked by the word 'Rangiriri' on the survey map] is beautiful river-plain farm land, and I had to puzzle why there would be anything there that would inspire a name implying violence,' he explains.

The word 'Rangiriri', it transpires, means 'sky of fire', or 'angry sky', and seems to be an obvious link to the Maori folktale and the 100 warriors who died so suddenly in the vicinity. As he says, the area today is quiet, peaceful farm land covered in lush grass. It wasn't always like this. Over the past 400 years the river has moved its course, looping a few metres away on its floodplain from that spot. Where cattle now feed, fish once swam and unknown craft cut through the water. Today, there is no obvious sign visible to suggest some disaster of long ago, yet the piece of Maori folklore suggested that there must have been a disaster. Hilliam reasoned that if there was an answer to the puzzle he appeared to have unearthed, then it may well lie below ground.

So he hired an excavating machine to dig down on the spot, but after reaching its maximum depth of 6 metres nothing of consequence was found. And, as well as that, because the works were taking place in moist, river-borne sub-soil, the hole began collapsing in on itself which caused the uneasy farmer to bring operations to a hasty conclusion before he lost his whole paddock. There had to be another way of resolving the problem.

Next step was to engage the services of a mining company, who from a sonar scan found something solid at last in the otherwise clear river silt, the length and proportions of which coincided with the shape of a ship! And a recently taken magnetometer survey (c. 1989) is expected to give more definite form to the radar echoes, enabling exploratory shafts to be sunk about the 10 or 12 metres required in a bid to confirm the presence and identity of solid objects around the ship shape – thought possibly to be cannon – which have also been detected.

Pieces of the puzzle keep coming to light. Further down the estuary some amateur fishers made another discovery. They were bringing mussels to the surface with pieces of pinkish wood attached to them. Further diving revealed larger pieces of the mystery timber. They turned out to be planking from a ship, attached to the curved bow frame. The method by which the planks were attached to the frame was square peg trundling unique to Spanish ships of the 16th century. Sections of the timber, bored through by centuries of Toredo worm, have been analysed and identified as *Lagerstromeia*, which occurs in a belt between southern India and the Philippines, where the Spanish had their base at the time the mystery Kaipara vessel was supposedly wrecked. It is thought that the section of ship found in the mussel bed is most likely part of the large shape found 10 metres under the mud further upstream, and that 'Rangiriri' and the 100 warriors dying suddenly are all intertwining elements of the one incident.

Here is one possible scenario: An unidentified Spanish ship sailed up to the northernmost reaches of the Kaipara Harbour – which is the same thing as saying the lower reaches of the Northern Wairoa River – some time between the years AD 1526 and AD 1530. It was challenged on the nearby beach by a large party of warlike Maori who would have had ample time not only to first notice the craft, but also to monitor its progress up the harbour. There would also have been time to assemble in numbers at a point where the vessel was

The galleon was used by the Spanish to transport people and materials to and from their colonies. The vessel was prone to capsizing when too many cannon were mounted aloft. (COURTESY OF THE SPANISH NAVAL MUSEUM, MADRID)

unable to proceed any further, either for the purposes of a friendly reception, or else a showdown. As was the custom of the day, a vigorous challenge was issued as the strange and frightening object drew nigh, except that this time there was an unexpected difference in the response. Instead of returning peaceful sounds and gestures, the fiery, hot-blooded Spanish captain thought the spirited haka a prelude to attack so decided to fire his cannon – either at the large group on shore, or else over their heads – in order to establish a quick mastery of the situation. To do this he had to bring the ship about to align his guns. It was a foolish thing to do under the circumstances. Many ships of this general period were top heavy because of the number of weighty cannon mounted too high, and more than one vessel capsized in those days while turning too quickly in a confined space.

One of the best examples of this type of tragedy is the Swedish ship *Kronan* at the battle of Oland in 1676. She turned too fast, heeled, capsized, *exploded*, and sank. It is likely the same thing happened to the Spanish ship in the Kaipara Harbour. Perhaps when it keeled over, either a cannon or two exploded, or else a seaman holding a lighted torch was precipitated accidentally into the powder magazine, thus causing a tremendous explosion. The ship sank and settled into the mud, part of the superstructure drifted downstream and came to rest in what is now a mussel bed, 100 warriors only metres away on the beach were killed in an instant by the blast, the sky was 'filled with fire', and for a while was 'angry' with smoke – hence the name 'Rangiriri' given to the spot. This explanation seems best to suit what has been discovered thus far in the area and only time will tell how close to the truth it really is.

Meanwhile, Spanish authorities have become so interested in the Rangiriri site that they recently sent out two archaeologists of their own to check it out. And they most certainly wouldn't have gone to such lengths without good cause. In an obvious deal between one country and the other, the whole matter has quickly developed from one of a totally speculative nature to something of much more substance. Also, discoveries already made have excited the interest of both the Spanish Ambassador to Australia and New Zealand, Dr José Luis Pardos, stationed in Canberra, and the Consul to New

Zealand, Sr Bartholomew Porta in Christchurch. Both have given hints that Spain might be willing to show a much more concrete interest in Hilliam's discoveries. Sr Porta has gone as far as initiating studies on his behalf at the Madrid Naval Museum, a conservative institution not given to issuing statements of a historical nature lightly. However, they have seen fit to state publicly already that 36 ships which set out from Spain between 1526 and 1566 did not return and that any one of them could have come to New Zealand. It's an intriguing prospect, and one which leaves the door wide open to almost any possibility. All this activity is certainly a refreshing change from the stance on these things which was held formerly.

Even though the Rangiriri wreck may have had most of its superstructure blown away by an explosion, the excavation by archaeologists of the similarly afflicted *Kronan* has shown that below decks everything more or less remained intact. Swedish coins, containers, medical chests and the like were recovered in remarkably fine order and this has raised hopes that similar material will be recovered from the Dargaville site. If one of the first pieces up is a cannon of Spanish manufacture, and the ship lying beneath the silt alongside the Kaipara harbour is indeed an old caravel or galleon, we can now look to the *literal* meaning of most of the old Maori folktales with much greater confidence.

Winnowing the Wheat of Folklore

What can we make of the many shadowy traditions which until now have largely been dismissed because of lack of detail, or because they had something of a fairy-tale ring to them? If we take just one of these, and treat it with respect, we might be surprised at the result.

In J. Polack's *New Zealand* (1838) a good example occurs:

> An indistinct tradition had been handed down of a houseful of atuas, arriving from the clouds; but with the exception of the dog having taken his passage in the aerial conveyance, and who was left behind to solace the people – nought else was preserved to refresh the recollection. (p. 269)

It isn't possible to get much more obscure than this. The vagueness in the story speaks of great age in a similar manner to other folktales which touch on matters relevant to our quest. In order to make any sense of Polack's 'indistinct tradition' though, we will need to turn it upside down and shake hard until something spills from it.

To more fully appreciate what it is saying, we must first create another similar hypothetical tale of our own – a process which we hope will not only magnify our understanding of the genuine story, but will also give us an idea how the folk stories we have today evolved into their present form.

On 15 February 1820, the British naval store ship *Dromedary* left Port Jackson in Australia bound for the Bay of Islands, after 'having got on board twelve bullocks and two timber carriages'. The ship was taking the Reverend Samuel Marsden and party to that area and the bullocks and carriages were for hauling spars out of the forest to be used as a backload for the return journey of the *Dromedary*. R.A. Cruise (*Journal of a Ten Months' Residence in New Zealand*, 1824) eventually saw the team of bullocks at work among the trees and wrote in his journal:

> The strength displayed by the bullocks when recovering, on a timber carriage, the spars, from the wood to the water's edge, drew forth the most unqualified expressions of surprise and admiration [from Maori]; people from distant parts of the country came to witness the extraordinary spectacle and returned with the most exaggerated accounts of the 'Karaddee nue' [kuri nui] or large dogs, the white men had landed on their island.

Here we gain from Cruise a number of things, including an insight into how some of the old-time legends might have been born. To Maori of the time, the spectacle of the bullocks at work was entirely new. It was impressive, and memorable. In fact it was the stuff epic fireside tales in an oral culture are made of. That it had, within days, already acquired some of the hallmarks of a legend is indicated by Cruise's words that the people 'returned [to their villages] with the most exaggerated accounts'. One more thing we learn from this story too is the fact that the meaning of the word 'kuri' was capable of being expanded to cover any four-footed animal. And that is something we need to bear in mind for later.

We'll stick with this story of the bullocks and use it as an illustration of what could have happened under certain hypothetical circumstances.

Suppose for the sake of our illustration that in 1820 the *Dromedary* was the first European vessel ever to come to New Zealand, and that those aboard her were the first white people ever seen by Maori. Further suppose that immediately after the spectacle of the bullocks at work the *Dromedary* and her people sailed away again and for the next 300 years after that there were no further visits by Europeans whatever. Then, in the year 2120, a vessel did return to the Bay of Islands. Her captain, in writing down all his observations in his journal, one day happens to hear a tradition about giant dogs, so his ears prick up and he faithfully records the story. But by then, after having passed down through so many generations, what is the story going to sound like? Will we recognise it? Based on the information that we have, and which the navigator doesn't, the journal entry would probably read as follows:

> An indistinct tradition had been handed down of a houseful of atuas bringing giant dogs with them. Obeying mystic words of command the giants quickly pulled the forests into the sea and nought else but a large patch of bare land was left behind to solace the people or to refresh their recollection of the event.

Now suppose another 200 years elapsed from the time of this entry, and it wasn't until the year 2320 that historians and writers discovered this particular tradition in the navigator's journal and began to pontificate as to its significance. What kind of comments could we expect them to make? That the 'houseful of atuas' was merely a poetic symbol to indicate the general dwelling place of the Maori gods? That the 'giant dogs' were simply types for a cyclone of more than usual ferocity which once flattened a large area of forest? That the story was simply a tale of retribution by one or more deities for some misdeed by the people long since forgotten? That it was a story cooked up by someone with a fertile imagination to explain a large area of treeless country? There is no end to the incorrect assumptions and interpretations possible.

But we know better, don't we? We are aware of the real events which were originally responsible for the navigator's tradition. We know that with a first European ship coming in 1820, white men would have been regarded as gods of a sort. We also know that in describing a fully rigged sailing ship Maori at the time wouldn't have had precise words to describe such a sight so that 'floating house', 'giant white canoe', and other phrases would have been pressed into service instead. We know also that the 'giant dogs' in the navigator's story were simply bullocks yoked together, and would have been termed thus for the simple reason that 'kuri' was the only word available to describe a large quadruped. And instead of the forests being pulled into the sea, as in the story, only selected trunks would have been dragged down to the water's edge with slowness, and with great difficulty. So our interpretation of the future navigator's legend is extremely simple because we know things the future historians and writers don't.

So to get back to the real tradition described by Polack. Its interpretation becomes simple also. All it is saying is that an as yet unidentified European ship appeared out of a dense fog – or else its vast sail area looked a bit like low-lying clouds – and that the fair-skinned occupants came ashore for a visit characterised by peace and goodwill rather than the normal bloodshed. We know this for two reasons. First, the words 'who was left behind' indicate the visitors were able to leave again. And, second, there was an animal involved in the story. As we shall see in other chapters, whenever this occurred there appeared to be an absence of bloodshed; the stay was often protracted even to the extent sometimes that the visiting white people actually had names bestowed on them. But not always. The purpose of the visit in the tradition we are studying would have been no different from the purpose in any other similar account. The need to land to pick up water, firewood, and fresh food of any kind for a scurvy-ridden crew was reason enough. Supplies of all kinds would have been at a desperately low ebb on *any* sailing ship reaching our shores in prehistoric times.

The words in the tradition about the 'dog' being left behind to 'solace the people' indicates that the eventual departure of the strangers was the occasion for some sadness among Maori, who didn't want to see them go. And the 'dog' was most likely not a dog at all either, but rather the usual pig or goat given in exchange for whatever supplies were picked up in the area. And that's all there is to it. There is no need to add in any mysterious elements or opt for long-winded and difficult interpretations. There are none.

When we approach other traditions in the same way, especially those much richer in detail, the process is something like winnowing wheat or oats. The kernels of truth fall at our feet, while the husks of unhelpful imagery are blown away by the strong winds of perception. What we are eventually left with is one truth – a simple account of a not-so-simple event which took place in prehistoric times.

From the very beginning of European-Maori contact, writers from the former group have been fascinated by Maori lore and tradition and have done their best to record what they can. The result for us today is a good cross-section of what must have existed in the very beginning. However, it is quite clear that for every piece of lore that has been saved, several others have been lost and, sad to say, are still being lost. Moreover, there are probably still undiscovered folktales about pre-1769 European visitors to New Zealand, either languishing in archives somewhere, or else firmly locked up in Maori mind. The discovery of such a gem by Anne Salmond in 1991 is a good example of this sort of thing (see below). But, even so, our hands are more than full with the material we do have, and still to be dealt with yet are tales which feature such things as white people coming up the Hokianga Harbour armed with muskets 'without locks' (Cruise, *Journal of a Ten Months' Residence in New Zealand*, 1823), and on another occasion up the Hokianga a boat's crew being 'cut off by the natives' (Cruise again), the white captain of a ship coming ashore in the Cook Strait area and fathering children (Beaglehole, *The Journals of Captain James Cook*, 1955–74), and also in Cook Strait a European ship which was 'beat to pieces on rocks' (Cook's *Journals* again), the various Rongo-tute stories – all essentially dealing with roguish, white-skinned ships' captains harshly treating coastal Maori (see Chapter 5), pale-skinned 'devils' in a strange craft fishing alongside Maori canoes near East Cape (Anne Salmond, *Two Worlds*, 1991), the Shag Point 'cargo' boat which brought 'pakeha things' to the South Island about 500 years ago (as told to J. Herries Beattie by the respected Teone Taare Tikao), fair-skinned strangers coming ashore in the northern part of the South Island wearing 'shiny coats that could turn off the Maori stone weapons' (Elvy, *Kei Puta Te Wairau*, 1957), to mention just a few of them.

This list of New Zealand's secret, alleged, pre-1769, non-Polynesian visitors is a surprisingly long one.

Special people are required to work on all this material – special people with perception and flair. People who, like Orbell, Evans and Hilliam, have what it takes to push back the frontiers of knowledge.

2

Maori Superstition and Quasi-humanoids

A Journey through the Spirit World

To assist further in distilling truth from Maori tradition we must now look at the matter of pre-contact beliefs – a task which becomes necessary because most of the material we have on pre-1769 visitors is couched in terms consistent with those beliefs and, therefore, likely to be of obscure meaning to some non-Maori.

The daily lives of old-time Maori were ruled by hundreds of unseen elements which had a profound influence on every facet of their waking hours. There were so many deities to appease. So many ogres and imps to be wary of. So many spiritual laws to observe. And so many spells and incantations to be on guard against. Occult forces were all-pervasive, and this totally coloured the perception of everything seen and heard – including fair-skinned 'gods' suddenly turning up in huge 'floating houses'.

Pre-contact Maori didn't have these things on their own of course. Members of pakeha society three and four hundred years ago were also ruled by a multitude of unseen elements which had a profound influence on every facet of their waking hours. They too had deities to appease, ogres and imps to be wary of and spiritual laws to observe. For them occult forces were all-pervasive as well, and if you broke the laws of pakeha tapu in those days you were likely to be burned alive at the stake! So old Maori beliefs were not inferior to their European counterparts. They were simply different.

What concerns us here is the manner in which the old Maori spirituality was used to mould the language of tradition because we need to understand this process as fully as possible. Hopefully, this chapter will provide some of this understanding. It will show how a knowledge of these things is a necessary component of our arsenal and that, without it, we would only be guessing. The problem is, however, that there is no clear-cut dividing line between fantasy and fact. We will have to grope our way along. But as the journey from one side of the spirit-world spectrum to the other proceeds, we will eventually cross the line and suddenly find ourselves among old Maori ideas and expressions which could only have been generated by contact with another race prior to 1769.

The following headings cover all aspects of the subject:

1 Atua
2 Tohunga
3 Tapu
4 Makutu
5 Aitua
6 Human sacrifice
7 Charms, spells, karakia, etc
8 Monsters and ogres
9 Spirit creatures and quasi-humanoids

These headings can be likened to bins of gold-bearing ore which we will shortly begin to process. Just how many 24-carat nuggets of fact are eventually separated out from it all, though, is another matter. This is something which will only become apparent with the passage of time.

Atua

The Maori word 'atua' did not originally mean 'god' in the sense that Europeans mean 'god'. 'Atua' was a word to describe any object of superstitious regard whether 'good' or 'evil', or whether flesh-and-blood human or ephemeral fantasy creature. It didn't seem to matter. So, for instance, when a sailing ship drew nigh to a party of Maori on the beach pre-1769, the fair-skinned strangers on board were initially regarded as atua simply because they were objects of 'superstitious regard'.

There wasn't a single, all-purpose 'good' god in ancient Maori society at all; a whole host of lesser deities were recognised and pressed into service instead. Some, like Tane and Tangaroa, are reasonably well known. But others like Haumia, the deity who presided over fern root, or Kahukura, the atua of the rainbow, were not so well known. Neither was Mokoroa, the atua who sometimes caused disease. And while there was not one 'good' god, except perhaps the shadowy Io, there was most certainly a malevolent one. His name was Whiro and he was the very personification of evil, and of darkness and death. He was probably equivalent to the European 'Satan'.

Normally, the atua was invisible. But under certain circumstances the tohunga could appropriate an 'arika', or a visible form, to a particular atua. A meteor or comet seen in the night sky was considered another type of visible form also. The sighting was known as a 'tunui'. Sometimes the tohunga carried around a 'potipoti', a small wooden box with a lid hinged with cords in which he professed to house an atua. But this could be dangerous. It only needed some unfriendly person to utter a 'tairo' and the tohunga would be instantly destroyed by the atua who was supposed to have been his friend. Much better for him to maintain a 'pua' at his sacred place. That way, the atua could alight on the post only when summoned. Or perhaps the tribe might have its own 'kawaka', an ordinary person fortunate enough to be the human medium of an atua. A person, who when not so possessed was known as a 'kohiwi', and who when in this quiescent state should not be confused with a 'tore atua', a woman who was lucky enough to have an atua for a husband.

'Kohiwitanga' was the name given to the visible habitat of an atua, and food specially set aside for the deity was either 'korotapu' or 'matana'. And then there were the emblems, or 'iorangi', belonging to the various atua and cared for by tohunga and other special people in the tribe. The 'amorangi' was carried at the rear of an advancing war party by the appropriate holy man and when placed in the path of an approaching foe was certain to bring disaster to them. Atua had their uses. But, more often than not, most appeared to be rather spiteful and it paid to be constantly on your guard lest you offend one of them unwittingly.

Tohunga

The tohunga was a skilled wizard, or priestly sorcerer, and a general custodian of the occult arts in each tribe. He was in charge of esoteric lore and had the responsibility of passing this knowledge on in the 'wharekura', or sacred learning-house, to hand-picked young men who were considered so valuable they weren't even allowed to go to war.

The tohunga was in charge of all spiritual protocol. He had the last word both on and off the marae. He recited 'makamaka', or special incantations, and had one for every conceivable purpose. He administered the laws of tapu and had the power and authority to place such things as 'makaka', for instance, on a human body to prevent it being eaten. Later, he was able to remove this and any or all the other restrictions of tapu with a 'whakamama' ceremony. He was often a 'matakite', able to foresee events, or he could be a 'mata', a medium of communication with a spirit. He practised 'huri kaupapa', or divination in its various forms, and was well versed in 'makutu' generally. But he was perhaps at his busiest in time of war where he always travelled at the rear of the advancing column.

Before battle he recited the 'mono' to disable the enemy, then the 'komahunu' to destroy their courage and self-respect. This was quickly followed by the 'koangumu' which would hopefully deprive the enemy of their strength. Finally, the 'tamoe' charm would be used to finish them off. Other charms resulted in a powerful blessing upon the weapons of the fighting men soon to be used. The 'ki tao' took care of a single spear, but the 'huru' was needed if all the weapons present were to be blessed simultaneously.

If things began to go wrong when the battle heated up, a quick 'whakakahurua' spoken on the run would effect an escape from the enemy by impairing their vision. And when it was all over there was the 'huri' ceremony to perform in order to remove any lingering tapu. The 'kawiu' was an enemy scalp taken home so that certain uncomplimentary incantations could be said over it. The tohunga may also have taken one or two enemy hearts back with him as well for similar purposes, or else to offer as food to a favourite atua. And later, a special oven called a 'rua iti' might be prepared and a 'kopani horua' incantation would be used to close up the oven once the spirits of the enemy had been lured into it.

There was almost nothing the tohunga couldn't do. He was generally held in fear by all.

Tapu

If we look to H.W. Williams' *Dictionary of the Maori Language* (first published 1844) for the meaning of 'tapu', there will be little need to go elsewhere for enlightenment. According to this authority, tapu was a state of being . . .

> Under religious or superstitious restriction; a condition affecting persons, places and things, and arising from innumerable causes. Anyone violating tapu contracted a 'hara' [an offence] and was certain to be overtaken by calamity. As a rule, elaborate ceremonies were necessary to remove tapu and make everything 'noa' [free from tapu].

Usually it was the tohunga who administered the placement and lifting of a tapu. And in some cases, the clever use of the device did benefit the community as a whole, especially when it came to protecting food sources. For instance, when the tohunga declared a newly planted kumara field tapu the not-yet-formed tubers became out of bounds to all. If someone did later take any for their own use without authorisation, the consequences could be disastrous, not only for the offender, but possibly for the crop as well. If the violation was a 'kurepe', the crop simply withered and died. It wasn't until the tohunga had conducted a 'pure' or 'mahu' ceremony that the vegetable became available for consumption.

Tapu could operate on a personal and on a private level also. When travellers arrived in an area new to them, they had no idea what local tapus there might be in force at that particular time. So to avoid accidental infringement it was necessary to perform a 'whakau', which involved depositing a twig or tuft of grass in a prominent spot and uttering the appropriate karakia over it. This act was insurance against penalties which might normally otherwise have been imposed.

A perceived penalty for a minor breach of tapu was known as a 'parahuhu', whereby offenders found that an enemy they were pursuing remained always just out of reach. However, there was one consolation. If people wished to gain ownership of any particular article, they had only to utter a 'tukutuku' – presumably in front of witnesses – to secure it. The only stipulation was that they bestow a personal name on the object.

Perhaps the strangest application of tapu was in regard to language, where particular words became sacred and it was forbidden to speak them. The word might be avoided because it entered into the name of a chief, for instance. The word 'wai' (water) is a case in point. If the chief's name was Waipuku, then the word 'wai' became totally tapu in that tribe while the chief held sway. Different tribes had their own tapu substitute words for 'wai' but 'mote', and particularly 'ngongi', are the best known. It didn't end there, however. *Any* word which had 'wai' in it was altered so that 'Waikato' became 'Ngongikato', 'wairua' became 'ngongirua', and so on. It was all very complicated. Even a modern lawyer would have trouble sorting out all the intricacies of the old tapu laws.

Makutu

A makutu was a powerfully bewitching spell or incantation. Even today the existence of such a device is a prominent feature of many societies but in old-time Maori hands it was quite deadly. The makutu could be invoked by tohunga or common citizen alike but when wielded by the tohunga it struck particular terror into the hearts of those towards whom it was aimed. The powers were not imaginary either. On record are eyewitness accounts by Europeans who saw them at work. Even the trees weren't safe apparently. In early Hawke's Bay a tohunga is said to have waved his hand over a tree which had displeased him in some way and the leaves turned from green to brown as people watched.

Makutu was used as a supernatural tool to benefit in some way the tribe or individual invoking it. However, it usually always involved entering the 'twilight zone', that ill-defined area where the laws of physics were temporarily set aside.

A 'takurangi' was a powerful charm used to cause a flood, while the 'apu' words could be relied upon to create an instant strong wind. A 'papa haro' was bad news for lands and forests: it destroyed their fertility. And if a 'whakamatiti' was invoked against some poor unfortunate person their limbs could be expected to dry up and wither away soon after. These makutu attacks against individuals probably worked better, though, if an 'ohanga' was used –

anything which served to connect the curse with the person involved such as hair, fingernails, and the like.

There were some defences against makutu. The 'tokoora' charm might on occasion nullify the effects of witchcraft, or a 'whakehokitu' could sometimes be relied upon to render nugatory any incoming supernatural blasts from another. But perhaps the best defence – for a man anyway – was the most unusual. Retracting the prepuce could be counted on to render most hostile makutu innocuous. This was 'titoi'.

Aitua

This word means 'evil omen'. Almost everything that happened to an individual in pre-contact Maori society was generally regarded as some kind of an aitua. Continuously, day after day, the most innocent and trivial of events was interpreted as a portent of something nasty. It is interesting to note here in passing that pakeha have always had their aitua too. Such things as walking under a ladder, spilling the sugar and leaving crossed knives on a bench are good examples.

All the great multitude of different Maori aitua had their own exclusive names but here we will only be dealing with an extremely small proportion of them to demonstrate their all-pervading nature. In a general sense, 'kato' was hearing a rat cry out, 'kotipu' was witnessing a lizard crossing one's path, 'umatupapaku' was noticing a halo around the moon, 'kaiwaka' referred to threatening clouds on the horizon, 'rua kanapu' was the act of seeing lightning flash over the hills, and so on. All these trivial events – and a thousand more – were thought to bring extremely bad luck to the person witnessing them.

On a personal level, to sleep frequently in the day time – 'whakawai' – was really courting disaster. To dream of seeing a person floating through the air wasn't much better. That was known as 'pekerangi'. If you talked unintelligibly in your sleep – 'kumanu' – or didn't repeat the words 'tihei mauri ora' (or similar) after each sneeze then you could expect to be in big trouble. Even a 'hui', an involuntary twitching of the limbs, was regarded as an aitua, as was giving way to fear – 'miti aitua' – to the extent that the mouth and throat became dry.

Perhaps the most surprising aitua came from the most unexpected of quarters – that of singing. Quite literally, it was dangerous to sing in old Maori society. The various slips one could make were just so numerous. For a start, you never sang alone. That was 'kohau'. You never sang without reason on the marae either ('taputapu ariki'), and singing while near the house out of doors ('konewa') was really asking for trouble. A 'tupaoe' was hearing strange voices singing at night. That was particularly bad. If you must sing you had to do it with others, but if your voice happened to be pitched above the others you might as well resign yourself to some sort of adverse event befalling you.

To be fair, though, there were one or two good omens to balance out the foregoing. For instance, if you threw out your arms while asleep ('ruru te takiri'), or stretched the limbs before realising what you were doing ('taiaroa'), you stood a chance of dodging at least some of the bad luck.

Human Sacrifice

In many societies the practice of sacrificing human life for spiritual reasons was part of the culture. Maori were just one of these societies. The 'toro-ngarehu' was sometimes killed at the time a woman's lips were being tattooed. The act was said to impart prestige to the operation. And when an important new house was being built the 'tumau', or what in effect was the human sacrifice for the occasion, was buried under one of the corner posts. When the tribe might be having rather a bad trot, and nothing had been going right for a while, it was most likely time for the 'ika paremo', a victim killed to bring good luck.

Most tribes kept a few slaves on hand for these ritual killings. And anyone innocently crossing the path of a war party was declared a 'maroro' and put to death immediately. It certainly didn't pay to be in the wrong place at the wrong time in old pre-contact New Zealand!

Charms, Spells, Karakia

As Williams says in his *Dictionary of the Maori Language*, the present-day application of the word 'karakia' to public worship is a recent phenomenon only. This means that, in the wake of this, the wider meanings have tended to become obscured – or even perverted. When Europeans first came to New Zealand this purely occult word denoted *any* form of words chanted in connection with a charm or spell to bring either benefit or protection to the utterer, or else calamity to his enemy.

For instance, in old Maori society a 'papaki' was recited by a man in order that the death or injury of the woman who had just rejected his advances would result. The karakia in those circumstances was a death-wish. Or if the disappointed suitor didn't want to go quite that far he could tone it down a bit and just invoke the 'ritua', a karakia charm to induce the woman to leave her husband quietly of her own accord. And there were plenty more karakia he could utter to help him have his way with the object of his affection.

If he embarked upon a second attempt at seducing her, the simple act of uttering the words of the 'tumata pongia' charm would render him invisible to the husband. This was a very necessary precaution. And since the whole escapade was likely to be a strenuous and strength-sapping one it would be as well to utter the 'tangaengae' while he was at it to confer vigour upon himself. If his scheme was discovered in time by the husband then a 'mahuruhuru' by the intruder would render him fleet of foot enough to escape. If his scheme wasn't discovered, a quick 'whakato' charm would induce conception. If the husband entered the scene at that stage now would be the time for a hurried 'kopani' to blind his eye. A 'haumaruru' would enfeeble him, a 'wetewete' would continue the process and a 'whakamoemoe' would cause him to be overcome by sleep.

Of course the enraged husband would be chanting plenty of karakia of his own during this process, with both pursuer and pursued each believing that their respective words were magic and that their petitions to the various atua and wairua would naturally be the ones to come to pass. They were probably simultaneously uttering the 'kuruki' or 'matapuru' charms, devised for the purpose of diverting threatened supernatural danger onto someone else, or else for warding off the effects of someone else's spell generally. If the husband did manage to catch up with his quarry, it would be time for he of the hot blood to intone the 'haruru', or possibly even the 'hono'. The first was a charm to heal wounds generally, while the second was especially efficacious when it came to fractured limbs. And this sort of thing might go on for days, and use up dozens of different karakia.

When not bickering over women, or fighting an enemy, there were plenty of spells and charms to invoke in order to assist in such endeavours as hunting or food gathering. The 'awe' stilled a storm that was being a nuisance, the 'tokotoko' dispelled the winds, the 'rotu moana' made the sea calm, a 'ruruku' prevented a tree from splitting when felled, a 'tua moe' was used by fowlers to lull tuis to sleep, and so on.

With the appropriate karakia a harmless-looking stone or piece of wood became an 'ara', or talisman, and with the 'hau', ordinary twigs became special in divination rites. The 'tamatane' was a bit more complicated. This karakia was uttered as part of the special preparation of an object as a charm to be cast at the person to be dealt with. There were, in fact, charms for every purpose, and karakia for every occasion.

Karakia in general go back very many centuries – so far, indeed, that many contain words of uncertain meaning found nowhere else. Many also contain words to which no known meanings can be ascribed at all. The significance of each is lost to us; the relevant information has gone to the grave with the old-time tohunga. As a result, any further enlightenment in this area now seems unlikely.

Monsters and Ogres

In the world of Maori mythology and tradition volcanoes scudded across the landscape, giants strode up and down the land devouring humans, people turned to stone, or else had fearful encounters with larger-than-life creatures of one sort or another. These monsters were to be found in the water, in the air, on the ground, or under the ground. No place was free of them.

Best known of the fearful Maori creatures would have been the lizard-like 'taniwha', a fabulous monster supposed always to live in deep water. Most lakes and deep river holes had their own resident taniwha, and Maori mythology – *not ever* to be confused with tradition and lore – is replete with tales of encounters with the beasts. The very idea of a dark, evil entity lying in wait in water to devour any humans who may happen to come along is wonderful raw material for a thousand tales of terror. And that's exactly what has happened over the years.

There were many other creatures to watch out for, however. There was 'Kaurehe', 'Maia', and 'Maero'. There was also 'Tuna Tuoro', 'Nauhea', and 'Ngarara'. Others, such as 'Tioro' and 'Kakarepo', probably lived underground. Some lived in the sea. 'Ratamoke' was one of these. So was 'Marakihau', 'Ngutuhue', 'Hore' and 'Matuarua'. Air-dwelling ogres to watch out for were 'Ririo', 'Pouakai', or 'Rauhamoa'. And there were plenty more.

It is just possible, though, that several of these 'monsters' and 'ogres' may well have had their origins with real and actual creatures. 'Pouakai', for instance, is described simply as a 'fabulous gigantic bird'. Could it have been *Harpagornis*, the extinct giant New Zealand eagle? This bird is known to have attacked and eaten moa. In the hundreds of years since the last one died did it slowly assume fabulous and supernatural qualities, and an increase in size? 'Hokioi' is another bird in this category. It too is both extinct and held in superstitious regard by Maori.

As for other creatures, the great 'Kumi' was an alleged fabulous reptile which instilled particular fear into the hearts of those who beheld it. But it too may have had quite ordinary beginnings. To help us understand this suggestion better, there is an account in James Cook's journal for 25 February 1777, in which he says in part:

Tiarooa tells us there are Lizards and Snakes in New Zealand of enormous size, he described the first as being round as a man's body, he said they would seize on and devour men, that they burrow in the ground and that they are killed by making fires at the mouth of the holes. We could not be misstaken in the Animal, as he, with his own hand drew a very good representation of it . . . (Beaglehole, 1955–74)

There is a mixture of fantasy and truth in this account. That Tiarooa drew the likeness of a real lizard-like creature for Cook there can be little doubt. Perhaps the sighting of a large tuatara at some time was the inspiration. And perhaps also the Kumi stories began with the sighting of nothing much more than a large lizard which lived in trees, and is now extinct.

Spirit Creatures and Quasi-humanoids

When we approach the Maori spirit world it shouldn't come as a surprise to find there was a whole culture woven around this particular subject also. Old-time Maori had a vast array of spirit creatures to deal with in their daily lives. The fact is, there was always some supernatural being or other to watch out for. Some entity that needed either dodging, appeasing or placating, or else just plain fleeing from, and whose wrath could be kindled by the most trivial of incidents. The area of the Maori spirit world is a complicated study, but secreted in its depths are nuggets we need to be on the lookout for if we are to further our knowledge of pre-1769 non-Polynesians in New Zealand.

The first aspect of this subject to be considered is the matter of hearing voices when there is no apparent visible source for them. Maori accepted such experiences as a normal part of everyday life, and sourced the voices to a wide variety of entities they believed existed all around them.

There were 'Orurua' and 'Parangeke', voices in the air. 'Punawaru' could be heard in running water, and 'Irewaru' was a spirit voice heard at night on the sea coast. However, hearing the voice of an 'Irirangi' was regarded as a bad omen. 'Haurakiraki' were familiar spirits, and if you wanted to communicate with the spirit of an absent person you need only repeat the 'takiura' charm to make such a thing possible. Te Reinga at the very north of New Zealand was the departure point for all human spirits making for 'keno', the underworld, but who knows where 'Kikokiko' – those malevolent demons who caused sickness – lived? Or any of the many other races of spirit beings who lurked nearby? There were the 'Rangipokohu', the 'Tiramaka', and the 'Tahurangi'. And how about the 'Mangamangiatua', the 'Porohete', and the 'Po Morikoriko'? Or the 'Karitehe', the 'Mareikura', or the 'Whatukura'?

Little is known of any of these 'races', or why there should be so many. Speaking about them was always difficult for Maori and it is likely our knowledge of them will never be complete. It could be that in the dim and distant past some of them may have been actual people of some description. Who knows?

'Wairua' was a collective term to describe all spirits, and the word could also be applied to any shadowy or insubstantial image whatever.

What about the two mystery words 'kehua' and 'taipo'? According to Williams, 'kehua' is a modern word which, like 'wairua', can be used to denote any ghost or spirit. 'Taipo' is even more mysterious. Ostensibly meaning 'goblin', which as we know is another pre-Cook way of describing Europeans, even Williams can't throw any light on its real meaning or beginnings. 'The word is used by Maoris believing it English,' he says, 'and by Europeans believing it Maori, it being apparently neither.' So where did it come from? And more to the point: *when* did it first come into use? Before Cook, or after?

Next we come to a whole group of different words which describe a whole group of different beings, and we find that going through all this material leaves a certain exciting after-taste. It becomes difficult, though, to sort out where fantasy ends, and where fact might begin. The key words are:

- motea
- pakeha
- pakepakeha
  pakehakeha
  keha
- paiarehe
  parehe
  patupaiarehe
  patuparehe

- pawhero
- korako
  korakorako
  koreko
  korekoreko
  rako
- kakarepo

- urukehu
  makekehu
  kehu
- turehu
  uru turehu
  Niturehu
- whakehaehae

Motea

This is an old word which means 'pale', or 'white-faced', and it's difficult to see how it was ever meant to apply to a brown Polynesian face.

Pakeha

'Pakeha' is a much maligned and misunderstood word, considered by some non-Polynesians to have certain unsavoury connotations, which of course it hasn't. Neither is the word a Maori form of the English 'bastard', as some persist in asserting. 'Pakeha' simply means 'foreign', or a 'foreigner', but not necessarily of the light-skinned variety. A Chinese from Canton, or a black from Soweto can just as correctly be termed a 'pakeha' by Maori as the white Europeans already living in New Zealand.

Pakepakeha, etc

Williams ponders whether the word 'pakeha' is related to this word in some way since both obviously are very similar. But while a 'pakeha' can have skin of any colour, a 'pakepakeha' cannot. Our word here first and foremost refers to 'imaginary beings resembling men, with fair skins'. It is a source of constant wonder that, long before Maori are supposed to have seen white people, most of their 'imaginary', and not so imaginary, human-like beings in tradition had fair skins and light hair. As we proceed along this line of research we will become even more aware of the fact. Ultimately, we won't be able to shake off the feeling that somewhere in Maori prehistory the two cultures met.

Variations of the principal word are 'pakehakeha' and 'keha'. This last word does have several other meanings but the ones we are most interested in are 'pale', 'dim' and 'whitish'.

Patupaiarehe, etc.

This word has loosely been translated to mean 'fairy', but such a translation falls short of the mark. A patupaiarehe was much more than a 'Tinkerbell' type of European fairy. The fact that it could be both malign or beneficent endows it with qualities not unlike those of ordinary human beings. One of the best descriptions of a patupaiarehe comes from Dr A.S. Thomson, who, writing in 1859 about Maori and their spirit world, stated:

> In some instances the spirits of their deified ancestors entered the bodies of lizards, spiders and birds; in other cases they became invisible human beings called Patupaiarehe. These spirits, which correspond to our fairies, imps, ghosts and goblins, were supposed to have had larger frames, and fairer complexions than men, to live in villages situated on the summits of lofty mountains, and amuse themselves by singing and playing on flutes. In the morning and in foggy weather these Patupaiarehe were sometimes visible to mortal eyes, and the terror they inspired made people afraid to leave their huts after nightfall; yet from them men were said to have learned the arts of fishing and weaving nets. (*The Story of New Zealand*)

Note how Thomson refers to patupaiarehe as 'invisible human beings . . . sometimes visible to mortal eyes'. And the bit about weaving nets is interesting too. Cook and his fellow-travellers in 1769–1770 more than once remarked about how Maori nets were woven 'in exactly the same manner as ours'.

Variations of the patupaiarehe word are patuparehe, paiarehe and perehe. All mean approximately the same thing.

Pawhero

This is one of a number of words in the Maori language which refer to either red or light-coloured hair – but in this case only insofar as these hirsute attributes apply to people. The restriction in its use is such that it would be incorrect to apply the term to animals.

Korako, etc

A 'korako' was strictly an albino, although there are those around who maintain that the meaning of the word could just as easily be extended to include any white-skinned person.

The different words in the 'korako' family have some interesting and subtle variations of meaning. A similar word, 'koreko' (or 'korekoreko'), does have 'white' for a meaning, and 'rako', which like 'korako' means 'albino', is in fact just a shortened version of 'korako'. Although related to 'korako', the word 'korakorako' is slightly different again. Here once more we come up against human-like 'fairies', 'imagined to be white skinned' (Williams, *A Dictionary of the Maori Language*, 1917), with the added refinement on this occasion that they could also sometimes be freckled. How did Maori know about freckles in the times before Cook?

Kakarepo

All we know about this word is that it is meant to denote a 'goblin' with ogrish tendencies. As we have already seen, the 'goblin' words are always worth taking a second look at in these contexts.

Urukehu, etc.

'Urukehu' simply means 'light-haired', but it was a name also applied to a race of light-haired, fair-skinned people who allegedly inhabited the East Coast area around Lake Waikaremoana many centuries ago and seemingly, also, right up to present times. When the noted author Mr T. Lambert asked a local elder towards the end of the 19th century who the Urukehu were, the reply was direct and simple. 'They were,' the old Maori said, 'a race of people who lived here long before the first Maori arrived from Hawaiki'. This idea of an ancient race preceding Maori is deeply entrenched in the area. (Those interested in more detail should consult Elsdon Best's *Waikaremoana – the Sea of Rippling Waters*, 1897.)

Best tells us that the local Tuhoe people 'pride themselves on being the direct descendants of the aborigines' found in the area upon their arrival. 'Tuhoe are,' he says, 'the remnant of a most ancient primitive race.' (A light-haired race.) Evidence for this comes from two principal sources. Tuhoe have preserved in incantations 'hundreds of words from some archaic language of the shadowy past', and, even today, there are more Urukehu in the north-eastern part of New Zealand than anywhere else. But the fascinating thing is that while Urukehu are beings from tradition and lore, rather than from mythology, and while references place them deep in prehistory, they are also alive and real in 1990s New Zealand as well. In an unbroken line their presence stretches back from today right past most of New Zealand's known yesterdays. In old tradition or recent written histories they have never been represented as other than human beings. What's more, they never have been reputed to possess supernatural or fabulous powers. In other words, they have only ever been ordinary people who just happen to have been in New Zealand an extraordinarily long time. So what are their origins? Here is what Eldson Best has to say about them generally:

> 'Urukehu' is the term applied to the singular and ancient type seen among the Maori people, whose peculiarities consist of a very light-coloured complexion, as that of an octoroon, and red or light-coloured hair. They have ever been numerous among the Tuhoe tribes, and would appear to be

the lingering but persisting remnant of some remote archaic type. (*Waikaremoana – the Sea of Rippling Waters*, 1897)

Does this describe an Aryan type?

Variations of the 'urukehu' word are 'kehu' and 'makekehu', 'kehu' indicating 'reddish', while 'makekehu' speaks more of 'light-haired' in much the same sort of way that 'urukehu' does.

Turehu, etc

According to Williams, 'Turehu' were 'apparently a supposed light-skinned race who came early to New Zealand'. Here once again we have the same basic idea of an early white race anterior to the Maori, expressed by yet another different word. A meaning of 'turehu' is also 'pale', and long before Europeans arrived in New Zealand 'uru turehu' meant someone who was light-haired.

Unlike 'Urukehu', who are not normally vested with supernatural powers, 'Turehu' have a certain air of mystery about them. But whether this was initiated by 19th-century European writers is difficult to say. J. Polack, for instance, in the verbose and pretentious style of his day, wrote a lot of words on the subject but didn't seem to say much. The following is a sample:

> At Piroa, or Doubtless Bay, on one of the most prominent hills, is said to reside Niturehu, a filthy deity, whose affection for red headed ladies and gentlemen . . . [and whose] . . . gout for red hair may be said to lend a colour to his actions; but those natives whose locks bear any resemblance to a vegetable red, invariably, on mentioning this deity, deny it, admitting their crinigerous covering is not absolutely black, but like some northern nations, whose tresses are said to resemble the golden sand of the Pactolus . . . (*New Zealand: Being a Narrative of Travel and Adventures*, 1838)

The word 'Niturehu' is a bit of a mystery here because the 'ni' part of it doesn't appear to occur naturally in Maori at all. It may be just an abbreviated form of the word 'nihinihi' (see Williams' *Dictionary of the Maori Language*, meaning no. 2).

Whakehaehae

This is one of the 'goblin' words. It seems fairly clear that the 'goblin' of Maori tradition may not necessarily have been a supernatural creature at all, although this will probably always remain open to some debate.

In John White's *Ancient History of the Maori* (Vol. 5, 1888), if we can take the account at face value, we gain some helpful insights into the pre-contact Maori concept of gods, goblins and all the rest of it. An eyewitness by the name of Horeta-te-Taniwha, who as a small boy went aboard Cook's ship at Whitianga in 1769, tells us that when the old men of the tribe first saw the *Endeavour* coming towards them they called it a 'tupua'. This is a very interesting word, embodying in its meaning several senses simultaneously: 'an object of terror', 'something which is strange', a 'foreigner', a 'goblin', or a 'demon'.

Another reason the old men dubbed Cook and his crew 'goblins' was the manner in which the visitors rowed towards the shore with their backs facing it. This could only mean that these people had eyes in the backs of their heads, so therefore they *had* to be goblins. Now because Cook is so well known, and because his visit to Whitianga is so thoroughly documented, we can dismiss all the talk of 'tupua' and 'goblins' and put it down to lack of previous knowledge. We know very well that Cook and his men were *not* goblins. But this doesn't completely solve our problem. What about the numerous references in Maori lore to earlier tupua and goblins? What are we to make of these? Were they Cook-like in appearance as well? Did they row towards the shore with their backs facing it too?

Perhaps the most fascinating and detailed of all the goblin stories is the piece of oral treasure discovered and translated in 1991 by Anne Salmond and Merimeri Penfold (*Two Worlds*, 1991, p. 62). Quite likely of pre-Tasman vintage, the story concerns an unspecified number of Maori canoes arriving at their favourite fishing grounds at dawn. Obviously some considerable distance from shore, 'they floated and let down their anchors, and began to fish for tarakihi'. When the sun rose 'a boat was seen paddling towards them, coming from afar off. It was a long boat, with many paddlers on either side and rows of people in the middle . . .'

The strange craft came straight towards the Maori fishers who, initially, were afraid. But when the newcomers began catching fish the tension lessened. Somewhat emboldened, Maori paddled towards where the fish were biting whereupon the strangers immediately began rolling up their lines, and after hauling up their anchor rowed off. 'In no time their boat seemed to rise up on the sea, it looked as if they were paddling in mid-air, and finally they were lost in the clouds'.

And the Maori description of these people? 'They appeared very strange. They were fairy people (turehu), misty-looking (punehunehu), fair (ma), pale, like albinos (ma korako), red, like red ochre (whero takou) – that was the way their faces looked. They were fairies again (patupaiarehe), evil gods (aparangi), still-born spirits (atua kahukahu), and whistling spirits (kowhiowhio)' – in fact almost the entire gamut of what could be considered fairy-tale folklore nomenclature has been pressed into service on this one particular occasion to describe early European visitors to the East Coast.

In Anne Salmond's story the most significant statement would appear to be that the white strangers were sighted 'many times, before and after that', as though their stay in the area was a protracted one.

We owe Anne Salmond a debt of gratitude for unearthing this rare Maori treasure. And we can be thankful that her attitude towards its value enabled her to say:

> Taken in conjunction with the 'Dieppe' maps of the mid-16th century that mark 'Cap Fremose', identified by some experts in historic cartography as the East Cape of New Zealand, and Hervé's controversial arguments about a landfall by a Spanish caravel just south of East Cape in 1526, this manuscript adds further interest to speculation about a possible Portuguese or Spanish 'discovery' of New Zealand.

Down-to-Earth Origins

As we saw under 'Monsters and Ogres', the origin of some so-called 'super-natural' entities may well be tied up in creatures no more exotic than ordinary birds and lizards. There may have been some sort of an element of Maori fear present to begin with, which, after the passage of many generations, would have made the creatures longer, larger, more fearsome, and otherwise endowed with qualities they never originally had. Basically, it seems fairly obvious that some of the most outrageous tales had very modest, down-to-earth origins indeed. A large fish seen planing the waves from the shore, for example, became a sea monster, and birds flying overhead at night were the source of many a tale of terror.

So if tall stories involving members of the animal kingdom can be shown to have such straightforward beginnings could not the same sort of thing apply to 'fairies' and 'goblins' also? Stories of patupaiarehe, urukehu, korako and turehu may very well have been inspired by Maori contact with lighter-skinned people centuries ago. And it may only be the passage of time once again which has invested these 'beings' with apparent mystic qualities never originally there.

Maori traditions speak of early sailing ships as 'floating houses', their occupants as 'gods' or 'goblins', and of the vessels as 'coming out of a fog or clouds', or else 'disappearing into the clouds'. In respect of these latter two phrases the descriptions are reasonably apt for a fully rigged ship displaying huge areas of white canvas. What else were Maori supposed to make of such a never-before-seen spectacle?

In conclusion, it should be noted that in this chapter we have not looked at every word in the Maori language which speaks of fair hair and light skin. There are a few others. The overall impression gained by studying them is that Cook and his men could not have been the first Europeans Maori had among them because there are just too many old words which seem to say otherwise. Apart from those already looked at, 'kiritea' means white-skinned and fair, 'moheahea' means light-haired, 'kama' means pale or whitish, and 'tauiwi' means both a strange tribe and a foreign race.

3

Do-It-Yourself Maori Folktales

A Beginner's Guide to Historical Discovery

The case for a pre-Cook, European presence in New Zealand rests rather heavily on oral tradition handed down to us by old-time Maori. This being so, we are faced with the task of retrieving every last little bit of it for study in case the one piece overlooked is the key of some kind, capable of deciphering other folktales, or else triggering off further research. Unfortunately, it isn't that simple. For despite what some may think, much valuable information exists which hasn't been found yet and although almost all is committed to paper somewhere the frustrating thing is that it isn't always recognisable. Not every relevant tale comes neatly packaged in a one or two-paragraph statement in some old book. In a few cases they are heavily disguised, and the material has to be wrested from its hiding place – often one or two words at a time – and often from a number of different sources.

Over the last 10 years we have witnessed the discovery of two new pieces of tradition which speak of surreptitious visitors to old New Zealand. Noel Hilliam found some puzzling words on an old survey map which, as we saw in Chapter 1, have triggered off an immense amount of activity. Anne Salmond discovered in the archives a piece about pre-Cook Europeans up the East Coast which had first to be translated from the Maori. Both pieces of tradition were there all the time. And both had to be worked for.

This chapter presents yet another piece of newly discovered tradition. I will show how awareness of it first arose, how from one cryptic word a whole story was built, and how further research into other areas was made possible by the finished article. This will be a beginner's guide to finding your own piece of tradition: a step-by-step, do-it-yourself manual for those interested in pushing back the frontiers of knowledge.

The Mysterious Mr Stivers: a Tale in the Making

It all began with a footnote in an 1820 book where we are introduced to a man known only as 'Stivers'. On page 107 of Lee and Kendall's *A Grammar and Vocabulary of the Language of New Zealand*, we find that Stivers is featured in an ancient waiata, and the line which carries his name – 'E tata te wiunga te tai ki a Taiwa' – not only speaks of a visitor who arrived pre-1769, who made an impression, and who left peaceably again, but also hints that, in the Northland area at least, everyone would have known exactly who Stivers was. The reference to him is a familiar one and begs the questions: if he was so well known, what other indications of his presence in New Zealand before Cook have survived to the present day? And why doesn't Stivers feature in the written record alongside such other early visitors as de Surville and du Fresne?

The Maori form of Stivers' name in the waiata is spelt 'Taiwa', and this sounds so much like the word 'taewa' – a common Maori name for potato – that consulting Williams' dictionary to see if there was a linkage seemed the obvious first step in tracking down our quarry. The footnote strongly implied a Taiwa/Stivers connection, but further confirmation of this was needed because, although we had the beginnings of a story, hard information was now needed to give it any sort of form. This wasn't long in coming. Further details were found in Williams' dictionary under the word 'taewa':

> **Taewa, taewha, taiawa, taiwa, taiwhu, n.**
> 1 Foreigner
> 2 Catarrh, cold . . .
> 3 Potato . . .
> NOTE – in view of the meanings and varieties in spelling above, it is not improbable that the word represents the name of one Stivers, who is said to have visited the Bay of Islands before Cook . . .

This one dictionary entry provided the confirmation sought. The waiata 'Taiwa' does indeed translate exactly into 'Stivers' and not only that, several new elements are now introduced as well. First, there are five variants of the Stivers name. This indicates a widespread knowledge among pre-Cook Northland Maori of the visitor and possibly, also, that he was in Northland a number of generations before 1769. It is reasonable to suppose that a word would require many years to evolve five variant spellings and pronunciations, and many generations over a large area as well. Second, Williams offers no other meanings for any of the five 'taewa' words which means that every time we come across one from now on it can only apply to Stivers and/or his introductions. Third, Stivers' name has become synonymous with the word 'foreigner'. This means he was non-Maori. Fourth, a secondary meaning of the taewa words is 'catarrh', or 'cold', which is perfectly understandable. First contact by Europeans with Maori invariably resulted in the transmission of new diseases by the strangers and nasal, bronchial and chest ailments seem to head the list in this regard. Fifth, we get a clue about the introduction of ordinary potatoes into New Zealand well before Cook. (This subject is dealt with at length in the next chapter.) Sixth, Williams in his note appears quite comfortable with the idea that there *was* a European in the Bay of Islands before Cook.

So where to now? Perhaps we had better take a quick look at the pedigree of this particular dictionary, and at the credibility of the man who compiled it. Having satisfied ourselves that both measure up we should then be able to move on with confidence and, hopefully, flesh out the bare bones of what we have already discovered.

The Williams' Dictionary

Writing in 1917, M.W. Williams outlined the set of ground rules by which he treated each new word encountered while working on the *Dictionary of the Maori Language*.

'Finally,' he wrote, 'there is the plausible guess, which is frequently used by the translator *but should be vigorously excluded from a dictionary*.' (Emphasis added.) So the 'taewa' word and its variants were incorporated into the work without having to resort to guesswork. And when Williams asserted that 'it is not improbable that the word represents the name of one Stivers', he was stating that on the evidence as he saw and understood it, such was most likely to be the case. 'It is not improbable' is a fairly strong statement. It is only one step down from proclaiming something as an actual fact.

Now although the 1917 Williams (Herbert) credits Kendall in 1820 with the information, there are deeper implications present. The original Williams lexicographer (William) lived among the same Maori as Kendall, and in the same general area, and it is inconceivable that he would not have independently consulted Maori elders regarding 'Taewa/Stivers'. The information would have been checked and re-checked. So with the calibre of at least two 'Johnny-on-the-spots' – Kendall in 1820 and William Williams, Archdeacon of Waiapu in 1844 – there would appear to be few grounds for doubting that 'Taewa' equals 'Stivers', or that 'Stivers' equals 'Taewa'.

For the moment then, let's accept it. Let's agree that Stivers the foreigner – the European navigator – came to the Bay of Islands before Cook, introduced potatoes, and probably one or two bronchial and chest diseases as well and that, all in all, he made sufficient impact not to have been forgotten in language, song, vegetable and illness, long after he had gone. For we know he did leave the country safely again. The line in Kendall's waiata tells us so. It speaks of the 'rolling billows' extending 'nearly as far as Stivers'; that is, the rear view of the his ship disappearing over the horizon.

So much for the Williams family then. What about the dictionary itself? It doesn't take long to determine that its credentials too are impeccable. After a century of trial and error, and after incorporating the valuable efforts of such people as Grey, Maunsell and Atkinson, the 1917 edition was the treasured end-product of a long evolutionary process in which Herbert Williams M.A. had finally managed to place between the covers of just one book the vanishing language of an entire race. The dictionary was now *the* authority on the Maori language. Gone were the deficiencies of former attempts at a Maori lexicon: the omissions of Hale, the transcriptional errors of Taylor, the padding of Tregear, the shortcomings of Colenso. Here at last was something definitive and authoritative – the benchmark for all future scholars who may have queries about Te Reo Maori. The 1917 edition was edited under the auspices of the Polynesian Society and was based on the earlier dictionaries of W. Williams and W. L. Williams. It was the fifth edition of the original which first appeared at Paihia in 1844. No other Maori dictionary has a pedigree even approaching it and the many adjudications it contains must now be considered the final word on each particular point, especially insofar as they touch on Maori word origins.

Stivers in the Coromandel?

It's time now to comb through the written record in the search for further clues. Starting at the beginning we find that on 12 November 1769, while at Mercury Bay, James Cook recorded in his journal details of a fortified Maori village which he, Banks and Solander had gone to inspect. Banks described the village as 'the most beautifully romantick thing I ever saw', and wrote its name down in his journal as 'Wharretouwe'.

Now, in the 51-year period between 1769 and 1820, those like Banks who attempted to commit the Maori language to paper were completely without guidance when it came to correct spelling and word and sentence construction, and all the other problems associated with trying to record a strange new language so that others coming along later could make sense of it. Cook's own journals are full of strangely spelt Maori words. And for 50 years after him, other European visitors also struggled as best they could with the language on paper too. The credit for eventually laying the foundations of a satisfactory orthography goes to Samuel Lee, Professor of Arabic in the University of Cambridge. It was he who collaborated with the missionary Kendall to produce the *Grammar* of 1820. And it was from this point on that the Maori language on paper took the form in common usage today.

But when Banks was told the name of the Mercury Bay village in 1769 he wasn't really quite sure how he should write it down. 'Wharretouwe' seemed the closest.

In referring to this name in more recent times, no less a personage than the late Professor J.C. Beaglehole has suggested that the correct modern spelling of this rather cumbersome-looking word should be 'Whare-taewa'; unfortunately, he made no further comment about its meaning or derivation(s). It is a matter of absolute certainty that the Professor, in his usual meticulous manner, would have made totally sure of his ground before 'going public' with this information, and that he was quite happy that 'touwe' did in fact equate with 'taewa'.

Therefore we can confidently state that since another reliable scholar (H.W. Williams, M.A.) has opined that all the meanings of the word 'taewa' are totally bound up with either the name of Stivers, or else the items he introduced, then Banks' 'romantick' pa must have had some connection with Stivers or his introductions prior to 1769. 'Whare-taewa' literally means 'the house, or abode, of Stivers', or else 'the house, or abode, of Stivers-introduced potatoes', or less likely, 'the home of Stivers-introduced diseases'. What it points to is that the same unidentified navigator who visited the Bay of Islands seems to have spent time on the Coromandel Peninsula as well.

The Northland Chants

The next reference of interest we come across is found in a couple of old Northland chants.

When J.L. Nicholas was accompanying Marsden to the Bay of Islands from Australia in 1814 he recorded the two chants as they were being performed on the deck of the *Active* by returning Bay Maori (*Narrative of Voyage to New Zealand*, 1817). As we have just seen, the Maori language had not yet been formalised on paper at that time so what Nicholas wrote down was his own phonetic version of what he heard. Both these gems of earliest indigenous literature appear to contain words of interest to our study. These are 'thowhy' and 'thowy'. The point is: do they approximate close enough to Banks' 'touwe' of 45 years earlier to be Beaglehole's 'taewa' of more recent times? If so, then the words thowhy, thowy, touwe, taewa, taiwa, taewha, taiwha, taiawa in the written record – while all synonyms for potatoes – are in fact adaptations of the one European word, 'Stivers'.

Nicholas tells us that the second chant he recorded was concerned with the difficulties associated with the planting and/or harvesting of introduced potatoes. He did not know the significance of the first chant. But since both share a 'thowy' word, it is likely to be an agricultural song as well because 'thowy' seems to be the nearest word to potato in either.

So what do the chants tell us? What new factors can we tack on to our ever-growing folktale because of them? For a start they are the third confirmation found so far which tie Stivers to the Bay of Islands. As well, they

```
Mārănghĭ tāhŏw nărnăckăh ūteeăh mĭtūhŭ rŭhŭrŭ
Mȳtānghŏ hō wȳ ūteeăh nărtăckŏ thŏwbȳ
        Nărtăckŏ thŏwȳ
He-āh-āh, ūteeăh—ūteeăh—ūteeăh,
Hē-āh-āh cārmōthŭ
Hē-āh-āh cārmōthŭ
Hĕ-āh-āh tātăpĭ
Tārhāh tātăpăr—tātăpăr—tatăpăr,
Hē-āh-āh tēnnă tōnăh
Hē-āh-āh tēnnă tōnăh
        Hē-āh-āh,
Kĭ-ē-ăh tēnnă tōnăh
Hē-āh-ăh tēnnă tōnăh
Hē-āh-āh kīkī, hē-āh-āh kīkī
Ah-āh kīkī, āh kīkī, āh kīkī!
```

J.L. Nicholas' 1814 phonetic transcription of a Maori potato chant. It contains the first instance in the written record of a specially created Maori potato word actually referring to potatoes.

speak again of the man's far-reaching influence on the local culture. Besides five words in the language commemorating him, one poetic waiata fondly featuring his name and a village named after him, here now are two chants further perpetuating his name. The feeling grows that all this is another kind of confirmation too. It took time for all these things to come about and the chants only firm up the idea that the visit of Stivers must have occurred *well* before Cook's arrival.

Stivers' Legacy: the Taewa Name

The next reference we come across has more potential than anything found so far. If taken to a logical conclusion, it could well lead to a positive identification of our friend Stivers. And, if it did, it would happen this way . . .

Ernst Dieffenbach wrote in his *Travels in New Zealand* (Vol.1, 1843, p. 220) of a gang of Maori roadmakers in Northland in 1840, who upon completion of a particularly arduous contract, sang this waiata of woe:

'Ka ngaro te purapura,
Te pata kai:
Etiki ka mate: ko Taewa ka mate:
Ko te Paki ka mate:
Ko te Matiu ka mate:
Ka ka po nei te manawa:
Ka tahuri au ki te reinga:
He poro kaki ka mate.'

Translation
'The tobacco is gone:
We have no food cooked in a pot:
Etiki is hungry: Stivers is sick:
Te Paki is hungry:
Matthew is sick:
All our good cheer is exhausted:
We turn back towards the Reinga:
We are sick for some food.'

This would appear to be the first reference in the written record to a Maori actually being named 'Stivers'. Some Maori parent must have been impressed enough by stories of the original bearer of the name to have christened her son thus – providing further confirmation that the favourable impression left by the original Stivers must have been considerable.

Of course, there is another possibility. If he was anything like other Europeans who came early to New Zealand, Stivers would not have been averse to taking unto himself a Maori wife. Which means that any resulting offspring may well have had 'Taewa', 'Taiwa' or 'Taiawa' as part of their name. The roadmaker just mentioned may even have had the same blood in his veins as our man himself. And he could also have had brothers and sisters, and a large extended family – all Taewas perhaps.

So we have opened up a whole new area of research. If one set of Maori parents named their son after Stivers, or if there were isolated families of Taewas around, did the idea spread? For instance, has the name survived to the present day? And if 'Stivers' people did exist now, what explanation could they give for the origin of their name? Would any of them know?

At first 'Taewa' was neither a Christian name nor a surname. It seemed to be the *only* name a person had. But since the appearance of Lee and Kendall's *Grammar* in 1820, where the written Maori language had been formalised on paper, the missionaries reasoned that in the interests of further orderliness the keeping of parish records demanded everyone have at least two names, a Christian name, as well as a surname. So, because it was such anyway, 'Taewa' appears to have quickly developed into a surname. From the 1820s and 1830s it became caught up in the initial recording process along with hundreds of other Maori names and cemented in place permanently.

A search of the country's 18 regional telephone directories and 97 electoral rolls resulted in the discovery of 36 different individuals all bearing variants of the Taewa name – 36 living sources of potential information. As enquiries among these people began, it was hoped that older members of the families concerned would be able to recall vague traditions of having a pakeha for a distant ancestor. And, at the same time, similar expectations were held as a search of genealogical records was begun. At the time of writing, however, no hard information has turned up and the process of enquiry continues.

Non Sequitur

So we appear to have reached the end of the road in the assembly of our folktale. English-language sources have little else to offer on either 'Stivers' or 'Taewa' and just as we thought we had advanced as far as it was possible to go with the matter something completely unexpected turns up. We suddenly find that early French writers had things to say about Stivers – things which are completely at odds with all the foregoing, and which raise different questions. We are pointed towards these 19th-century French writers by Robert McNab, who in his *Historical Records of New Zealand* (Vol. 2, 1914, p. 230) says:

> From French sources another reference is found in M. Hombron's *Aventures des Voyageurs* (Paris, 1847, pp. 380 and 381). This reference is interesting from the fact that Hombron considers de Surville to be 'Stivers', who, according to the Natives, had visited New Zealand before Cook.

Is Hombron here saying that de Surville was in New Zealand twice? Before

Cook, and then again alongside him in 1769? Or is he simply saying that the Stivers tradition arose entirely from de Surville's only visit here in 1769? Where did he get his information, and what grounds does he have for proposing such a linkage?

J.B. Hombron was Dumont D'Urville's chief surgeon aboard the *Astrolabe* on the 1839–1840 expedition, and seems to have been just as handy with his pen as with bone-saw and scalpel. In his book *Aventures les plus curieuses des voyageurs coup d'oeil autour du monde . . .* mentioned above, he simply says: 'Surville est probablement le navigateur dont le nom est resté dans la memoire des naturels, sous le titre de Stivers' (de Surville is probably the navigator who remains in the memory under the title of Stivers) (p. 380). No real elaboration follows the statement and we learn nothing new about *why* he thinks what he does. With a little further digging we find that it isn't even an original thought. It was Dumont D'Urville in 1825 who seems first to have put the idea forward in the notes he prepared for his manuscript work *Les Zélandais histoire australienne*.

Carol Legge has transcribed and studied this manuscript and on p. 302 of her thesis on the work (1989) we find these words from D'Urville: 'Les vagues roulantes vont presqu-aussi loin que Stivers', and in a footnote on the same page: 'C'est un homme, qui, dit-on, a visité la baye des Iles avant le Capitaine Cook; tout dit bien de croire que c'est Surville.'

Legge says that in 1825 D'Urville was simply adding to Kendall's 1820 statement about Stivers, saying only he *thought* de Surville was probably Stivers. Then she raises the questions: 'Was Dumont D'Urville the first Frenchman to say this? Could there possibly be a mention in Rochon's *Noveau Voyage à la Mer du Sud*? If Stivers is *not* mentioned by Rochon, the source of Hombron's 1847 information automatically becomes Dumont D'Urville alone. The feeling at this stage is that Hombron is not worth considering further on this matter. He was merely parroting D'Urville's statement of 22 years earlier in *Les Zélandais*.

So all the French have managed to do is throw a temporary scare into us. Because it is not at all difficult to demonstrate that de Surville and Stivers were two completely different people:

- de Surville was *never* at the Bay of Islands.
- Stivers was *never* anywhere else (except perhaps Wharetaewa)
- de Surville left behind a smouldering resentment among far-north Maori. He was viewed as a kidnapper, and left no cause to celebrate his visit whatever.
- Stivers impressed Maori, to the extent that numbers of people adopted his name.
- Nowhere else in the entire written record is there the vaguest hint that de Surville and Stivers should be linked. It seems to have been just one person's casual idea that another thought he would repeat in passing.

A Dutch Stivers?

The French experience does have a positive spin-off for us. It has inspired a quest among other nations for any information *they* may be harbouring on Stivers. Enquiries directed towards various maritime institutions around Europe provided one predictable response, and one with distinct possibilities. The French mentioned de Surville in the same breath as Stivers again, but it was the information offered by the Dutch which surprised. The Director of the Netherlands Scheepvaart Museum said:

> We have found two V.O.C. (Dutch East India Company) captains called 'Stuyver', a Jan Stuyver, who sailed with the ship *Ouderamstel* in 1764–1765, and Klass Stuyver, who sailed between 1756 and 1766.
>
> . . . it is possible that one of them made an interasiatic voyage and somehow got lost. To be sure of anything, a lot of archival research needs to be carried out . . . There were some ships lost on homeward voyages in the Indian Ocean around 1760, but my guess is that if it was a Dutch ship (in New Zealand waters some time before Cook) it would have been privately owned by burghers of Batavia, because they were not as experienced sailors as the V.O.C. employees, and also, they could have made far more adventurous voyages than V.O.C. directors would have allowed their own men. Unfortunately in this case it is very difficult to find anything about such a ship.

The Director implies that not knowing about secret mid-18th-century, burgher-backed voyages from Batavia to this part of the world doesn't necessarily mean they didn't take place. Lack of knowledge results from the fact that such enterprises 'were rarely made public'. The Director is completely open-minded about the prospect of the Dutch being in New Zealand before 1769 (post Tasman) and goes on to provide details of where documentary evidence and proof of this is most likely to be languishing.

So was our Stivers a Dutch sea-captain? And is 'Stuyvers' merely the Dutch spelling of 'Stivers'? Perhaps Kendall got it wrong when he wrote 'Stivers' into the manuscript of his 1820 *Grammar*. Perhaps it should have been 'Stuyvers'. These differences in spelling prompt us to research the name itself, and its origins, in case there is anything new to be learned in this area.

The Stivers Genealogy

Thanks to the impressive resources of the local genealogical society freely made available it is soon possible to uncover all the detail we need on the Stivers name. We learn that it is one of a group of fine old English surnames which come bursting out of the Middle Ages in company with a dozen or more related surnames which all stem from 'Stephen' (he of the New Testament). Hence Stivars, Stevers, Staver, Stives, Stiverson, Stiverd, and so on. However, as we shall see soon, Stivers is not exclusively an English name. It was also known in France and Scotland.

The very first record of a 'Stivers' to be found anywhere in the world relates to one Thomas Stivers of Northampton, England, in 1540. Thereafter, in what appears to have always been a very scanty and sparse line, only about half a dozen other 'Stivers' people appear to be on record for the next 200 years.

The same resource also reveals that in the enormous holdings of the Genealogical Society of Utah are actual details of the worldwide comings and goings of all the Stivers and related families from about 1750 onwards. There are hints of loose groupings of anti-British French families, strange amalgams of Franco-Scottish Stivers people, and of some of these people playing a large part in precipitating and supporting the American War of Independence in the 1770s. It all needs studying in some depth to determine whether any of these particular wealthy and dissident Stivers people from Europe sailed anywhere near New Zealand on their way to what was later to become the United States of America.

The Tale Complete

And so we come to the end of our folktale-producing exercise. From a word here, and an idea there, we have gathered together many elements of a tradition which has always been there, but never like this in one place before. We have also developed a strategy to solve the various mysteries which usually come as an integral part of stories like this. And we are confident that there is every chance of a breakthrough with it. So what does our newly assembled piece of folklore read like now?

'Some time before Cook first came to New Zealand in 1769 a European navigator by the name of Stivers sailed into the Bay of Islands. Either French or Dutch, his visit was characterised by peace, and his impact on Maori was considerable. He introduced the common potato, and these were named by Maori after him. He also introduced bronchial and chest diseases, and his name became synonymous with foreigners generally. After he left he became something of a poetic figure, featuring in waiata and chants. Because of him, five new words with three different meanings were introduced into the Maori language, and in honour of him some local people adopted his name as their own. He may have visited the Coromandel Peninsula, where his reception was also friendly and memorable because a village there was named after him.'

Can we believe all this? Or is our folktale just a house of cards?

The fact is that our folktale can't be any more than a house of cards until hard evidence turns up to prove otherwise. But we can't let this deter us from pressing on. The task has hardly begun yet and we can thank Anaru Reedy for showing us how to proceed further. In his 1993 book *Nga Korero a Mohi Ruatapu*, he reminds us of something many people seem to have lost sight of: the existence of a vast New Zealand literary treasure largely unpublished, and largely ignored until recently.

He is referring to the works of 19th-century Maori writers from every iwi who since the 1830s produced a 'voluminous' body of literature comprising letters, reports, essays, histories, songs of every kind, newspapers and periodicals. He says that much of this written taonga is preserved and accessible – some in libraries and other institutions and some in private collections.

David Simmons (*Journal of the Polynesian Society*, Vol. 73, No. 2) tells us that the Grey collection alone consists of over 9800 pages of manuscript of which less than 700 pages have been printed. Almost all is written in the Maori language, and very little has been translated.

There is no reliable catalogue of all the unpublished Maori material in existence. No one really knows how much there is. The grand total could be in the vicinity of several hundred thousand pages – or more, and probably constitutes one of the largest sources of untapped information about early New Zealand we have.

The only requirements for the do-it-yourselfer seeking to explore all this material are an innate curiosity and a knowledge of the Maori language. And if Te Reo Maori is not one of your strong points, then consider doing something about it. Thus equipped, you'll be ready to embark on one of the last great intellectual voyages of discovery remaining in this country. Who knows what you'll find. You may even unearth proof that James Cook was not the first European to step ashore on to New Zealand soil. In fact you could unearth anything.

So why leave the task to others?

4

Creative Speculation as a Research Tool

Posing the Potato Question

There is a hint of underlying madness in the idea that from ordinary potatoes we may be able to extract information which points to a pre-1769 European presence in New Zealand. Yet in the next few pages that is exactly what I am going to do.

In his book *Tuhoe* (1925), Elsdon Best tells us that when a Maori woman in pre-contact times failed to produce children in the years immediately following her marriage she often resorted to a rather curious practice. Believing herself to be barren, she would dress up a potato and then begin nursing it as though it were a child.

Getting more specific, he relates the story of a woman called Moenga who had to cease using one of these potato soothers because she unexpectedly fell pregnant and therefore had no further need of it. A son was eventually born and, overcome with joy, she named him Tama-riwai, or potato son, in memory of the object which had formerly been her baby substitute.

Now Tama-riwai features in Bay of Plenty genealogies and folklore and Best was able to say of him that 'he cannot have been born later than the year 1750'. And what we can say, also, is that Moenga his mother is unlikely to have been the first woman to use a potato in the way described above. Which appears to mean that Bay of Plenty Maori had potatoes (*Solanum*) in their possession many decades before Cook arrived.

This is not the only indication in the Best writings of potatoes in New Zealand before 1769. In his article 'Maori Agriculture' (1925), he says:

> It is worthy of note that many natives maintain that certain varieties of the potato (*Solanum*) were known and cultivated by them, *prior to the arrival of Europeans*. [Emphasis added.]

And again:

> In the Bay of Plenty district it is a popular belief that the 'aroaro' and 'rokoroko' varieties of potato (*Solanum*) were cultivated there *prior to the arrival of Europeans.*'

And once more:

> Tutakangahau, of the Tuhoe tribe, stated that, in pre-European times the Maori cultivated the 'uhi', which resembled the kumara in growth, but *tasted more like a taewa*, the introduced *Solanum*.

In each of these instances Best was quick to offer reasons why he thought there couldn't have been potatoes in the country prior to Cook's arrival. The idea didn't rest at all well with him – despite having been told by numerous Maori that such indeed was the case.

Getting away from Best we find others also claiming pre-European potatoes in New Zealand. In G.M. Thomson's book *The Naturalisation of Animals and Plants in New Zealand* (1922), (quoting A. Hamilton) he says:

> De Surville was, with Cook, supposed to have been the introducer of the potato to the Maoris of the North Island and the northern part of the South Island. *Many old Maoris contend that 'taiwas' (potatoes) were known and largely cultivated before the advent of Europeans.* [Emphasis mine once more].

So what can this mean?

If there were potatoes here before 1769 – as these quotations seem to be indicating – it can only mean that some European was handing them over to the Maori well before Cook arrived. There is no other way seed potatoes could have entered the country. Maori didn't voyage overseas to get them. The tubers were brought here by someone else.

In Chapter 3 we studied a shadowy figure by the name of Stivers who is alleged to have done just this, but further progress in unravelling this and other potato mysteries is difficult because there is so little to go on. All we have for certain is a nagging doubt that all is not well. And it now becomes our task to find out why.

Much of the information gathered on Stivers is largely the result of careful speculation, and it is only by speculation now that we can hope to make any further progress with this matter. Some will be aghast at this proposal. The idea of linking the word 'speculation' with 'historical research' would be unthinkable to them. However, a close look at dictionary definitions will be enlightening at this point. True, the broad meaning of the word is to 'conjecture on a given subject without knowing all the facts'. But consider the secondary meanings: to 'think', and to 'study', to 'reason', to 'ruminate', to 'consider', to 'reflect', and to 'deliberate'.

When you don't know much about a subject and you're very keen to find out about it with little in the way of specific information to guide you, what's wrong with thinking, studying, reasoning, ruminating, considering, reflecting and deliberating in an effort to find out more? What's wrong with 'speculating'? It isn't a dirty word. Frank Whittle used creative speculation to develop the jet engine. Henry Ford came up with the V-8 engine because of it. Neither had hard facts to begin with. Both started with a radical idea. And I am going to attempt a resolution of the potato puzzle by the same method.

Word Clues

The only hard fact we have to begin with is that scattered throughout the written record are hints that potatoes may have been in New Zealand long before Cook arrived here. Beyond that we know little, and will just have to break new ground if we are to progress any further. From the hints just mentioned, of course, comes the inference that an unknown navigator must have been here before 1769 giving seed potato to Maori, and this gets us right back to Stivers again. While dealing with this person the thought arose – was he the only pre-1769 European who may have given potatoes to Maori? Could there have been others? If Maori commemorated the event once by introducing five new words into their language, are there other new words capable of telling us something else? Did they do it again? Were other early Europeans remembered in Te Reo Maori in the same way Stivers was because of potatoes – or other items – contributed?

There's only one way to find out.

Our first task is to compile a list of every known word in the Maori language pertaining to potato varieties and culture and then study them for clues. It shouldn't take long. There can't be too many words involved. If potatoes *had been* introduced by Cook in 1769 there wouldn't have been time for a multiplicity of such words to accumulate in the language anyway. After all, other 18th-century introductions such as cabbages, turnips and tobacco had each attracted less than a dozen different names during the introduction process, so why should potatoes be any different?

However, the search for potato words is to develop into a major saga and poses a number of new questions which wouldn't otherwise have occurred to anyone to ask. Potato words prove to be everywhere. Soon the list grows to 20. Then to 40. Then 60. We begin to realise that we are on to something. Surprise follows surprise as we find ourselves knee-deep in potato words.

Potato words in the Maori language up to 1917
This list is provisional; a final list could well reach 120 words.

1 *Existing words extended in meaning to include a variety of potato*

hiwai	ngangarangi	piho	raukaraka
kapa	papaka	popoia	repe
karamu	parareka	poranga	ropi
kimokimo	pata	pungapunga	uhi po
koparapara	pau	putawa	wiri
maori	peru-kokako	rape	

2 *Existing words extended in meaning to signify some attribute of potatoes, or activity connected with planting, tending, harvesting, preparing, cooking or storing potatoes*

huahou	kotiro	pukonohi	takuru
keretewha	kukari	punaunau	taroa
koiri	ngangatawhiti	rangirua	tauhere
kopiha	puhina	rua tahuhu	wairau
koropiha	puhua	rumaki	
kotete	pukanohi	taeka	

There are dozens more. *Too many.* Without trying very hard we soon have 70 different words, and then 80. So what's going on? They start to thin out a bit by the time we get to 90, and even though realising it is most probably not an exhaustive and definitive list a grand total of 94 different words is finally attained. It's quite difficult to come to terms with this huge number because there is no conventional explanation for them. Current wisdom has Cook introducing potatoes to New Zealand in 1769–1770 along with a variety of other vegetables at the same time, and at intervals during the next few years. There just wouldn't have been time for potatoes to have acquired 94 different names in the short interval between Cook's last visit and the arrival of the missionaries when everything was recorded on paper.

So why do potatoes stand so far apart from all other European-introduced plants insofar as the number of Maori names for them is concerned? There

---

3 *Specially created words for potato varieties. These particular words had no other meaning before 1917*

aroaro	kotuku-tawhiti	parewahine	taeaka
huakaroro	kotuku-tea	piakatoa	taewa
huamango	mahetau	porakorako	taewha
huarewarewa	maitaha	puahinahina	tahore
kapana	manerau	raparaparuru	taiawa
kaparapara	papake	raparuru	taiwa
kapetopeto	parakokako	raramu	taiwha
karuperera	parakonekone	riwai	waeruru
koropuna	parakotukutuku	rokeroke	waiararo
kotipo	parawhewhe	rokoroko	

4 *Specially created words for some attribute of, or activity connected with, potatoes. These words also had no other meanings before 1917*

kamora	konononono	mokoti	wari
katero	kotero	pukupango	
kokari	makanga	tamahou	

Total number of words in the Maori language associated with 'potato': 94

has to be a sound reason, and the only logical answer seems to be that they must have been here far longer. What else are we to think?

We find encouragement for such a notion when we begin to make a few comparisons. For example, how long have Maori had gourds in New Zealand? It must have been a long time – perhaps as much as 1000 years. In relation to his archaeological work at the moa-hunter campsites on the Wairau River mouth, Dr Roger Duff offered the opinion that one of the small items excavated was a calabash stopper. This means, firstly, that gourds were more than likely being grown in the South Island, and, secondly, that they were growing there almost 1000 years ago. And yet, significantly, for the entire period of the Maori calabash-gourd culture, which included everything remotely connected with the plant and its products, only 73 words have survived to the present time – 21 fewer than potatoes, which allegedly have been in this country only one-fifth of the time. The same applies to taro. This is admittedly a vegetable whose cultivation may have been confined to more northern, warmer areas, but it has nevertheless come through to the present day with only 53 words – 41 fewer than potatoes.

When we consider the other staple items used over the last 1000 years by Maori, such as kumara, eels and flax, potatoes with their 94 words do not lag anywhere near as far behind as they ought. There are 210 flax words, 210 kumara words, and 152 eel words. And, further, if we average out the number of words for the five staple items over the 1000 years (i.e. flax 210, kumara 210, eels 152, gourds 73 and taro 53) we get 139. So that potatoes at 94 for an alleged 220-odd year presence are not all that far behind the average figure of 139 for a more certain and provable 1000 years.

The argument could be advanced that potatoes became such an indispensable part of daily Maori diet during the period 1770 to 1820 that every family in the country soon had their own potato plot. But it wouldn't have happened overnight. It could have taken years for this to happen. And when it did, the distribution of such plots, and the way they would have cut across so many tribal boundaries where so many different dialects were spoken, meant it was only natural that words pertaining to potato culture should proliferate apace. Which on the face of it is quite plausible. However, it falls flat as a proposition because of another factor working hard against it. Hand in hand with the establishment of potatoes in every nook and cranny around the country went another plant – tobacco – which quickly became even more indispensable than the little white tubers.

The Tobacco Factor

A.S. Thomson wrote in 1859:

> Tobacco smoking was one of the earliest customs introduced by Europeans. Even before . . . 1840 smoking tobacco was almost universal. Natives without their pipes are uncomfortable, they never leave home without them, and rarely squat without lighting them . . .

W.R. Wade found in 1838 (*Journey in the Northern Island of New Zealand*) that on a visit to Mokoia Island in Lake Rotorua, Maori '. . . even made their own pipes, and grew . . . two varieties of the tobacco plant'.

Robert McNab is just one of the many other writers to tell us that tobacco soon became a universal currency as well. Purchases were made with tobacco, and debts settled in the weed. In *The Old Whaling Days*, just to quote one example, McNab talks about a ship's captain who rowed across to Kororareka to purchase a spar. The captain found one 37 feet long for which he paid ' . . . 36lbs of . . . tobacco'. Other writers give the value of everyday commodities in tobacco also, to the extent that the point isn't worth labouring any further. It wasn't until European settlements became established much later that a general switch was made to potatoes as a means of exchange for much coveted metal goods and fabrics. Stories of Maori supplying much of early Auckland with dray-loads of the tubers are well documented. One of the reasons for all the 'horse-trading' and bartering was that coinage of the realm was in such chronic short supply that growing your own money in the form of tobacco – and later, potatoes – was seen as the best answer to the problem.

With tobacco being such a valuable commodity, and with the 'natives' being so 'uncomfortable' without it, it would have spread around the country at least as fast as potatoes. If a conflict ever arose as to whether tobacco or potatoes should be planted in the ground available, tobacco is likely to have won out. It was worth too much not to be given precedence in most cases.

The distribution of tobacco plots was widespread too, and they cut across tribal boundaries where many different dialects were spoken, just as potatoes did. But the basic, bottom-line crunch fact remains. Tobacco acquired less than half a dozen Maori names during the whole establishment process whereas potatoes picked up a total of 94 different words. It is a huge imbalance, and once again we find ourselves asking why. It should have been the other way round. Tobacco should have led the way with a multiplicity of names because of its dual addictive and negotiable characteristics, and the fact that it so thoroughly pervaded every little corner of New Zealand with its presence. But it didn't lead out in this way and we are left with a real head-scratcher as a result.

Derivations of the Potato Words

We know that five of the 94 potato names (i.e. taewa, taewha, taiwa, taiwha, taiawa), pertain to one alleged pre-Cook visitor (Stivers). So what about the other 89? Are some of them hiding something too? We will have to concede that some of these will be variants of the same word in a few cases – such as 'puhina' and 'puhinahina', 'pukanohi' and 'pukonohi', etc. Some will be temporary localised substitutes while the natural word for potato in the area was rendered tapu for some reason. Some could conceivably stem from the odd sealer or whaler post-Cook. Some words will denote a skin colour (pukopango), or of flesh (piakaroa), or size (parawhewhe). Some words could equally have applied to kumara cultivation, and may in fact have actually begun as kumara or taro words and later had their meanings extended to cover potatoes as well because of the similarity of the three tuberous husbandries. Examples of such words are 'koiri', which means to plant potatoes, but which once probably applied to planting kumara (although Williams' dictionary doesn't specify this), 'konononono', a term applied to watery and waxy potatoes, but which could also have been used for kumara and/or taro, and 'kopiha', which is a pit for storing potatoes, but which once was also a taro pit.

A few words may have originated with an incident in tribal history – but who's to say? Some examples in this category may be 'kamora', which are potatoes spoiled by exposure to the sun, and its ally 'mokoti', which are potatoes which have lain in the sun and turned green. 'Kokari' are new potatoes and 'wari' are potatoes spoiled by frost. The list goes on. So where did these words come from? What did they originally signify? They had never been in the Maori language until potatoes came along. They seem to have appeared out of thin air, yet there has to be an explanation for their existence.

Even after taking all the above factors into account, plus the fact that potatoes would have been one of the most widely distributed and widely used of all introduced plants (except perhaps for tobacco – and there are less than half a dozen Maori tobacco words), a sizeable list of mystery words remain. 'Taeaka', 'wari', 'katero' and 'raramu' are just four examples. By checking a completed list of Maori potato words it will be seen that 49 of them have been specially created to deal with this supposedly new introduction by Europeans. And we have to ask ourselves just why there are so many such words.

A study of the catalogue of Maori potato words doesn't appear to offer much help either – at first. The 94 words on the list can be subdivided as follows: 22 are existing words in the language whose meanings have extended to include some attribute of, or activity connected with, the planting, tending, harvesting, storage, preparation or eating of potatoes; 23 are existing words which have been appropriated for naming potato varieties; 10 have been specially created to designate some attribute of, or some activity connected with, potato culture. And a huge 39 have been specially created just to name specific varieties. It is the combined total of these last two – 49 – which becomes our hunting ground. All are neologisms with one-off meanings. So what are these meanings?

The New Words

There are one or two clues. Williams tells us that in the beginning Maori were using words in conversation they thought were from the English language, whereas Europeans were using the exact same words believing them to be of Maori origin. Neither group was correct, and this mutual word abuse in the early days has remained largely unexplained until perhaps now. Williams also often admits that the meanings of many Maori words are obscure, or unknown, and because of this we may never know the circumstances of their origin, or what they signified. But explanations for at least some of these things may be hiding in a completely unexpected quarter after all, especially with regard to the 49 newly created potato words. Could it be that a percentage of them are the pre-Cook Maori forms of ordinary European words and proper names; that is, European words apart from English ones, that is? Have they defied recognition for so long because the words concerned are from the Dutch, Spanish, Portuguese or French languages, and were picked up and modified into Maori before 1769? We already have a precedent for this sort of thing – our friend Stivers. This pre-Cook European visitor to New Zealand has no less than five of the 49 specially created potato words to his credit, which demonstrates quite nicely that the naming of potatoes by Maori must have been a process which began before 1769.

To firm up this idea further, we can do no better than refer to an incident which took place during Cook's first visit in 1769.

The *Endeavour* anchored in Tolaga Bay on the East Coast for the week 23–29 October, and during that time there took place a free exchange of material goods between one race and the other. One of the items Cook gave Maori was potatoes, and referring to these later, the Turanganui chief Te Apaapa-o-te-rangi said:

> The parareka [potato] was obtained there, that which is called waeruru, the papake, and wiri, that is all those potatoes.

This is a very significant sentence – revealing and filled with hidden implications. It really needs to be read at least half a dozen times before its true sense and meaning becomes apparent. Te Apaapa is not saying here that Cook's potatoes were the first on the East Coast, or that Tolaga Bay was the place where potatoes were first introduced. There is no hint of that sort of thing at all. He is merely specifying, out of the dozens of varieties known at that time, which particular ones were dropped off on that one occasion – i.e. 'waeruru', 'papake' and 'wiri' – and nothing else. At the time of telling, parareka was just another general term to describe potatoes collectively – like taewa. Of the three varietal words, 'waeruru' is the only one recorded in Williams' Maori dictionary as a named variety whereas both 'papake' and 'wiri' are absent. This either suggests that Williams missed them, or that the two words have only a very limited application in one particular valley or river system in the Tolaga Bay area. 'Wiri' is an existing word whose meaning has been extended to cover a specific variety of potato and 'papake' appears to have been specially created. It has no other meaning in any part of the country.

Going deeper into this matter we find that potatoes may not have been the only European-introduced plants present in New Zealand before 1769. Turnips and cabbages were two others, but we only mention them here briefly because their story lends yet more support to the notion of a very early potato presence in this country.

Elsdon Best says that the word 'pora' was used by old-time Maori to denote turnips, and that the respected authority on ancient Maori lore, Teone Tikao, told him that it was a prized food plant 'grown by my ancestors in olden times. They possessed the pora *long before Europeans reached this land*'. [Emphasis added.]

Checking Williams for light on this word produces a pleasant surprise when we find that four of its principal meanings are significant for us. 'Pora' can be either a 'large ocean-going ship', something which is 'foreign', a 'stranger', and a 'wonderful person'. Does this explain the introduction of turnips into pre-Cook New Zealand? Does the 'pora' word commemorate the visit of a large sailing ship commanded by a foreign stranger who was a wonderful person? As in the case of Stivers, was the newly introduced vegetable named on the spot to mark the event? Except that, in this case, was the new name called into being to mark the circumstances of the *event*, rather than the *name* of the leader of the Europeans at the time? If so, it underlines the fact that when early Maori stated that they had turnips, or potatoes, or any other non-Polynesian item prior to the arrival of Europeans, they really did have these things. And just because the notion doesn't rest well with the accepted and orthodox view it doesn't mean it is invalid.

Approximations

But we've been digressing. Who else apart from Stivers may have brought potatoes to New Zealand before 1769, and had the event commemorated by Maori naming the tubers after the particular mystery donor concerned? Anyone? Or no one? We must get back to the list of 49 enigmatic Maori potato words in an effort to find out.

Some of the 49 words may have been created by Maori to approximate the sound of a European name; others, to approximate an event. So what would happen if we attempted to reverse the process? What if we tried to come up with European approximations for some of the 49 one-off Maori words we have managed to isolate on our list?

For example, to play with just a few:

1. Could Kapana be Cabana, or Captain, or Cap'n?
2. Could Katero be Carter, or Cartier, or Carteret?
3. Could Taeaka be Diack, or Dyak, or Striker?
4. Could Kokari be Corkery?
5. Could Takuru be D'Cruz?
6. Could Tahore be Charlie?

Other suspicious words such as 'kotipo', 'manerau', 'raramu', 'kamora' and 'mokoti' would probably require a rather intimate knowledge of several European languages to establish any further connections.

For instance, what about the word 'potato' itself in some of these languages? While handing over the tubers to Maori the pre-1769 donor may simply have uttered the word for potato in his own language and this could have stuck – probably in an unrecognisable form. A Dutchman would have spoken of 'aardappel', a Spaniard 'patatas', or 'papas', a Portuguese 'batatas', and a Frenchman 'les pommes de terre' (or an abbreviation of one sort or another). And for those who favour the idea that the mystery wreck of Ruapuke Beach may be of Tamil origin, how about 'urulaikizangu'?

Checking with the list of Maori potato words doesn't really offer a lot of light. There doesn't appear to be anything there resembling the Tamil word, or the French, or the Dutch. But there was a diminutive variety of potato known to old-time Maori as 'pata', and another called 'papa-ka', and a number of others all starting with the prefix 'para', or 'pare', suggesting a Spanish or Portuguese connection, but apart from that – nothing yet.

Hidden among the vast welter of Maori folktales are references to at least a dozen undocumented non-Polynesian visitations to New Zealand before Cook. Is Stivers one of them? Have the names of the other personalities involved been right under our noses all along? The word 'taewa' appears to be a potential key of some kind, capable of dramatically unlocking some of the secrets of old New Zealand's prehistory. It could almost be like a South Pacific Rosetta Stone. If this is so, Stivers stands in our prehistoric background, a shadowy figure with outstretched arm and finger pointing, trying hard to tell us something. But dare we believe what he is saying? Is he *really* fingering his furtive contemporaries? Are the names he is pointing to connected with the same non-Pacific people who feature in Maori folklore? Only time, and a lot of hard work, will tell.

At about this stage in our look at potatoes in early New Zealand an outrageous piece of speculation arises concerning their approximate introduction date:

> If it took Maori 1000 years to accumulate 210 kumara-related words (or 210 flax-related words – it really doesn't matter), how long did it take them to accumulate 94 potato-related words?

No? Oh well. It was worth a try.

Forgotten Stores

Finally, on a completely different tack, but still sticking with pre-1769 potatoes in New Zealand, we must now consider the matter of the discovery and digging out of certain 'rua', and other ground pits in which potatoes were stored. For some reason many of these were abandoned and forgotten around the country. A hapu may have laid down potatoes for future use and then been driven out of their homeland, or even annihilated, and knowledge of the stored potatoes lost. One such in the Turangi district was found to contain wizened-up potatoes packed in straw, this latter having long since decayed away to almost nothing. The potatoes were found to be at least 165 years old based mainly on the last known date of Maori occupation of the area. When planted some of them actually grew. There are thousands of such undug potato pits around New Zealand and there is no reason why some of them shouldn't contain ancient varieties of potatoes brought here some time before 1769 by a person or persons unknown.

The discovery of just one of these would validate everything written in this chapter.

5

The Ship of Rongo-tute

The Rongo-tute Stories

The most widely reported indication of a pre-1769 European in New Zealand relates to a shadowy figure known only as Rongo-tute to old-time Maori. But although most traditions depict him as a rogue, and often describe in detail how his ship is seized and his crew killed and eaten, not enough information is ever given to identify either the man or his country of origin. There are further problems too. So many versions of the tale have been handed down to us – all placing him in different time-slots and at different locations on the New Zealand coast – that it is difficult at times not to conclude that there may have been more than one of him.

Captain James Cook was first to record one of the stories. In 1774 he wrote of an earlier unidentified ship in Cook Strait, and again in February 1777, expanded on the theme in much greater detail. The visit in this case was calculated by Professor Beaglehole to have occurred in 1764, and was an extended one.

In *Wairarapa – An Historical Excursion* (1976), A.G. Bagnall writes:

> This story is the origin of the tradition of the ship of Rongotute. The attraction of a good-sized mystery of this kind . . . is almost overpowering . . . until we can confirm the Wairarapa tradition by some identifiable relic or by the still possible discovery of some ship which did not return to base Rongotute and his vessel must stand in question.

What Mr Bagnall is unlikely to have known in 1976 is that hiding beneath the sands of a beach not too far north of Wairarapa is an unidentified wrecked ship which could well be his 'identifiable relic'. But more of this later.

In 1859 A.S. Thomson (in *The Story of New Zealand*) spoke of a 'European vessel commanded by a man called Rongotute' visiting the 'southern part of

In John White's Rongo-tute story Maori smashed willow-pattern plates from the doomed ship and made neck pendants from selected fragments. The figures on some pieces were not unlike certain trees known to Maori with the result these imitation hei tiki were dubbed 'Te-upoko-o-rewarewa' – 'the head of rewarewa'. None is known to have been found in an archaeological context.

(COURTESY DARYL GRIGGS)

the North Island . . . about the year 1740', and 'that from some cause the natives killed the crew and plundered the vessel.'

In 1878 Rev. J. Buller (*Forty Years in New Zealand*) recorded a tradition which again featured the arrival of a European ship 'commanded by one Rongotute'. The ship in question was plundered, the crew destroyed, and the date given for the incident 1640. This is not a misprint because Buller goes on to say that 'two years after that date, a Dutch navigator called Tasman came to anchor, but did not land.'

In 1888 the first of a new batch of Rongo-tute material began to appear in print. John White, Elsdon Best and Percy Smith did their best over a period to flesh out the bones of the traditions with newly gathered information which often went into great detail. White featured Rongo-tute as 'evil', and suggested that the capture of his ship and the destruction of his crew were almost in the nature of a self-inflicted disaster. The event occurred at 'Aropawa', and after dealing with the crew Maori allowed the ship to drift on to the beach where it was stripped of everything useful. (See *Ancient History of the Maori*, Vol. 5, 1888, pp. 120, 121.)

Percy Smith believed that the Rongo-tute disaster happened either at Palliser Bay in the Wairarapa, or else in Queen Charlotte Sound, and put forward a novel explanation for the tradition. Quoting from an 1825 account of the voyage of the *Coquille* he hoped the information provided 'may perhaps throw some light on the story' (*Journal of the Polynesian Society*, Vol. 8, p. 203):

> It is said that a Scotch gentleman, who was inflamed with the idea of civilizing the New Zealanders, embarked in 1782 with sixty people, and all kinds of indispensable articles for cultivating the soil; his project being to establish himself on the banks of the River Thames, or in Mercury Bay, and to teach the natives the art of cultivation, but no news has ever been heard of him since he sailed.

An interesting one, but why would someone bound for the Coromandel be nosing around the Cook Strait area?

In 1912 Elsdon Best elicited further information from contacts in the Wairarapa which introduced new elements to the growing file on Rongo-tute. According to this version, Rongo-tute's ship was driven ashore at Te Kawakawa by a southerly gale, and there were survivors. The sailors managed to rescue a barrel of flour and set about making bread or damper 'which astonished the natives' so much they later tried to do the same thing themselves. And then the situation began to deteriorate for the hapless castaways. In 1912 a Maori elder was hardly going to admit that his not-too-distant ancestors had killed and eaten dozens of white men but Best observed that 'it is extremely probable' that this is indeed what did happen. Other details given by the informant would seem to confirm this anyway. Apart from hearing that the ship was ransacked Best was also told that three of the survivors 'had put to sea in a boat and gone up the east coast'. What else would they be fleeing from except imminent death? We are not told which 'boat' the three escaped in. Whether the ship aground on the beach refloated itself on the high tide, or whether a longboat on the deck was pressed into service, we simply don't know. Whatever the case, the three headed up towards Hawke's Bay and apparent oblivion. Or did they?

Mention should be made at this stage of an ancient shipwreck for which no known corresponding tradition among local Maori has ever been found. Waimarama Beach in Hawke's Bay is a mecca for holiday makers and surf-lovers from all over New Zealand but its vast expanse of finely groomed sand conceals many mysteries. Deep below the surface are buried forests, moa graveyards hectares in extent, a hodge-podge of centuries-old human remains and artefacts, assorted ironmongery and relics from a whaling station, a lost greenstone hoard, and at least one shipwreck.

At this spot where the Waingongoro Stream flows on to Waimarama Beach in Hawke's Bay, generations of children have built sand castles unaware that a few metres below them an unidentified shipwreck lies entombed.
(COURTESY DARYL GRIGGS)

Known to only a few old-timers, this wreck is not recorded in any of the shipwreck books, and has never been identified. Generations of children have built sand castles above it, and countless picnics have been enjoyed not six metres away from it, with all being completely unaware of what was hiding beneath them. Two or three times each century a Cyclone Bola-type storm exposes it, and the ancient rows of crude wooden ribs temporarily on view on these occasions bear mute testimony to some disaster of long ago. Could it be the Rongo-tute ship of Best's story? We'll never know until someone makes a serious attempt to identify it.

Shiploads of Smelly Foreigners?

You would expect some discrepancies in the various Rongo-tute stories, but not on the scale encountered, and not with such conflict and variety. To begin with, dates given for the incident range from 1640 to 1740 to 1764 to 1784 – and all points in between. Rongo-tute's ship was either washed up by a storm, seized by Maori when at anchor then set adrift, beaten to pieces on rocks, set alight, and so on. The event occurred variously at Aropawa, Queen Charlotte Sound, Cape Palliser, Te Kawakawa, and other places not named. Sometimes there were survivors. Sometimes not. Sometimes the crew was killed and eaten immediately, while on other occasions all was peace and love. Cook's Rongo-tute, for example, lived ashore with a Maori wife who bore him a son!

The more research done on the Rongo-tute material the more it becomes patently obvious that there was more than one Rongo-tute. And that rather than referring to a specific person, the word was originally conjured up to describe a whole *class* of people – a class distinguished by certain characteristics which set them apart from Maori. When we further consider that in the Maori language the word 'Rongo-tute' is used *only* in connection with early European navigators – and nobody else – the next step becomes obvious. We must now attempt to define just exactly what Rongo-tute signifies – what information, and what subtleties, old-time Maori intended should be enshrined in the word. Such an exercise will quickly reinforce the idea that the appellation does indeed reflect a class of person, and will also make the acceptance of a multi-Rongo-tute scenario easier to accept.

White gives 'news of the expelled' as an English equivalent for 'Rongo-tute' but this is not at all convincing. We have just hinted that the word most likely applies to a class of persons, rather than one particular person, and even though this is only speculation there is some strong reasoning behind the idea.

'Rong-tute' is obviously made up of two distinct and recognisable words. First, 'rongo', having four meanings:

1 Apprehend by the senses (hear, feel, smell, taste – but not sight).
2 Obey.
3 Tidings, report, fame.
4 Peace after war.

Secondly, 'tute', also having four meanings:

1 Shove, push, nudge.
2 A charm to ward off malign influences.
3 A quarrelsome cock pigeon.
4 The male of the tui bird.

Put together, 'rongo' and 'tute' are obviously trying to tell a story, and we can easily explore a few of the possibilities involved if we can first accept that the two words are nothing much more than 'triggers' placed together for a specific reason. In modern society we don't consciously need such devices because we have books to yield up any information we may require in a hurry. But in old Maori society the mind had to be stimulated by a trigger word (or words) which could quickly produce in great detail a whole story, or the recollection of any particular set of circumstances by the simple process of triggering off the memory banks of the subconscious. And since 'rongo' and 'tute' placed together are associated in Maori tradition exclusively with white men in ships we will confine ourselves to this area only.

If we take the first meaning of 'rongo' – i.e. to apprehend by the senses – and then settle on the sense of smell as being the one spoken of, we have to ask ourselves next what it was about the first European ships encountered that caused Maori to bestow a name which might imply an offensive smell. Was it that approaching the vast (to them) ship from downwind that it *did* smell? Of human waste, for example? Then should 'rongo-tute' have been more correctly rendered as 'rongo-tutae'? The ship which smelled of excrement? Or the people who smelled of excrement? Has the word 'tutae' been subsequently misinterpreted into an erroneous 'tute'? And was 'rongo-tutae' or 'rongo-tute' – originally used as just a general term to describe all fair-skinned visitors in ships simply because they smelt different? Confirmation for this idea comes from another source. East Coast Maori in their pre-Cook traditions referred to shiploads of Europeans as 'pakehakeha' (or its equivalents). The word 'kehakeha' in this context means 'an offensive odour' and 'pa-kehakeha' means literally 'the smelly inhabitants of a fortified place' (in this case a ship).

The second meaning of 'rongo' is 'obey'. If we couple this with the first meaning of 'tute' – shove, push, nudge – or its extended form 'tutetute' – jostle and hustle – it's not hard to imagine sailors jostling and hustling about the deck obeying orders from whomever was in command at the time. 'Rong-tutetute' could easily have been shortened later to 'rongo-tute' in much the same way as 'pakehakeha' became 'pakeha'.

A third possibility is to take the fourth meaning of 'tute' – a male tui – and put it together with 'rongo': to apprehend by the sense of smell. And what could we make of this? Perhaps the thing about early European ships that stuck most in the Maori mind – apart from the smell – was dress. If the officers on board wore black uniforms with white collars, or any civilians present also sported black frock-coats with white collars, it's not difficult to see how the fourth meaning of 'tute' could apply. The white-collared strangers could easily have evoked for Maori a picture of the male tui bird with its white throat feathers, so that 'rongo-tute' in this case would refer to the 'smelly tui-like creatures'.

Whatever the true meaning of 'rongo-tute' it seems fairly clear that it was designed to cover a group of people rather than any one specific person, so that the so-called 'ship of Rongo-tute' is in all probability a descriptive term which is more likely to have signified any pre-Cook European ship and its complement. Moreover, it's hard to escape the idea that somewhere along the line the idea of an offensive smell played a large part in calling the name into existence.

Post-Cook Rongo-tute Incidents

Rongo-tute incidents didn't end with the Cook visits of the 1770s. Why should they? Maori weren't going to alter their behaviour and way of life just because of a brief encounter with Cook. A visiting ship which became stranded and wrecked in, say, 1806 wouldn't necessarily have been treated any differently from one which might have come to grief in 1706. The record shows this. In fact if we study Rongo-tute lore for the period *after* Cook's time, we are going to gain a very clear perception of how these things probably were in the hundred years or more *before* Cook came. Let's look at one or two examples.

In 1806 the brig *Venus* was seized in Australia by a mixed bunch of mutineers, deserters and escaped convicts, who eluded immediate capture and subsequently turned up at the Bay of Islands. Here they entered on a career of pillage and kidnapping of Maori women. They 'committed evil on the Maori people' – to echo the words of a much earlier Rongo-tute tradition – and 'enraged' them with 'the evil of their ways'. It had all happened before of course – a number of times – and Maori seemed to have a set agenda for dealing with this sort of thing. In accordance with ancient lore everything cast ashore on their tribal territory became their property, whether a ship accidentally wrecked or a visiting one boarded and purposely run on to the beach. And this included foreign humans and all their possessions as well. In the case of the *Venus* – which is a perfect example of a post-Cook Rongo-tute incident – this time-honoured procedure was observed as usual. The ship was eventually captured, allowed to drift on to the sand, plundered and stripped, set ablaze to recover all metal objects, and the crew of 12 killed and eaten.

Even as late as 1838 it was still going on. In that year the French whaler *Jean Bart* was boarded by Maori at the Chathams, the vessel pillaged and burned, and the entire crew – said to number 40 persons – was killed and eaten.

The *Wairarapa* ran aground on Great Barrier Island on 29 October 1894. Of the 251 people on board only 130 survived and were found by local Maori and given every assistance. Had the incident occurred 43 or more years earlier the outcome might have been altogether different.

(COURTESY AUCKLAND CITY LIBRARIES)

It wasn't until 13 years later than the Rongo-tute era really came to an end. On 3 June 1851, the French corvette *L'Alcmene* came to grief near Hokianga under circumstances which, had the event occurred a few years earlier, would almost certainly have ended in disaster. But owing to the influence of the missionaries, and a growing understanding of European attitudes and values among Maori generally, the cycle was broken at last on this particular occasion. Hokianga Maori rendered every possible assistance to the wrecked Frenchmen. Later, the French government saw fit to publicly commend the Hokianga people for all their efforts on behalf of the sailors.

The record shows that from Cook's last visit right up to 1851, there were 22 confirmed Rongo-tute incidents, with three or four others being inconclusive, yet suspicious. Of the 22 ships involved 8 were pillaged and the crews massacred, 4 were pillaged and burned with the crews somehow managing to escape, and 10 were merely pillaged some time after being wrecked. In the post-Cook period total destruction and death was the fate of 36 per cent of all ships which came to grief on our shores prior to 1851. This figure matches almost exactly the situation as outlined in tradition where one-third of visiting pre-1769 European ships and their crews met a sticky end. The documented material this side of Cook is thus seen to confirm the traditional material for the pre-Cook period.

Oral Maori tradition dovetails so neatly into our own written record that ancient Rongo-tute stories are able to take on an overwhelming air of authenticity which makes them quite difficult to ignore.

6

The Seven Mysteries of the Korotangi

The Long Flight of a Lost Bird

The story of New Zealand's most enigmatic relic – the Korotangi – is a succession of interwoven puzzles which defy resolution. Carved in the likeness of a bird from a piece of dark green serpentine rock, the Korotangi was hailed by Maori when found in the 1870s as a genuine and long-lost treasure of their ancestors who were said to have brought it in the *Tainui* canoe from Hawaiki. Measuring 26.5 cm long from the point of its beak to the tip of its tail, and weighing just over 2 kg, it was supposedly found in the roots of a large manuka tree which had been toppled by high winds. The tree was growing in a disused rua (storage pit) 'somewhere between Kawhia and Raglan' and the original finders of the relic were said to be 'members of a native tribe'.

The first name which can definitely be linked with Korotangi is that of Albert Walker, a European drifter whose word and actions appear not to have always been entirely above suspicion. Walker is generally conceded to be the one who obtained the object from its Maori finders, despite the fact there is no direct confirmation of this. All we know is that at a certain point in time in the 1870s it was in his possession, and that he gave conflicting stories about how he had acquired it. One of these was that he had purchased it on board a New Zealand coaster. Whatever the truth of the matter, it does seem that Walker alone knew all about the circumstances of the carved bird's discovery – and perhaps even its production – and that most likely he took this secret to the grave with him.

Soon after it came into his possession, Walker placed the stone bird in the hands of a Major Drummond Hay, Cambridge, for safe keeping. Hay was a well-known collector of local artefacts and, although the Korotangi would have represented the most spectacular and exclusive piece he had ever seen, his reaction to it was only lukewarm. There could have been two reasons for this. Firstly, Hay might have realised at the outset that the bird was not of Polynesian origin, or else stumbled on to the truth regarding its true origins – and consequently soon lost interest in it. Secondly, he may have been too ill to care one way or the other because a short time later he suddenly died.

Walker then sold the relic to another prominent Cambridge resident, Major John Wilson, J.P., who was married to a Maori woman named Te Aorere, and for whom – some people assert – Korotangi was really intended all along. Wilson paid Walker £50 for the bird and is on record as saying that had the price asked been £500 instead of £50 he would have gladly paid it for so unique an object 'attested', as he believed, 'by the best native evidence available'. Rightly or wrongly, Wilson firmly believed the Korotangi to be a genuine Maori relic of the past, and that Maori generally had recognised it as such. In adopting such a position he was going much further than Hay before him.

The 'best native evidence' Wilson referred to was a succession of Maori dignitaries who had come to Cambridge to see the Korotangi for themselves. An unnamed chieftainess appears to have been first to recognise the object for what it was and who, upon first seeing it, bowed before it and greeted the find with song and tearful expressions. It was she too who helped to spread the word of the reappearance of the fabled bird lost for so many generations and now apparently found again. The song sung by the old lady appeared to be known in all parts of the country in different versions, and even 19 years before Korotangi was found Sir George Grey had published a version of it in his 1853 *Poems, Traditions and Chaunts of the Maoris*. There appears to have definitely been a widespread tradition in Maori lore of a lost bird, but whether Korotangi is the one may never be proven.

The old chief Rewi Maniapoto came to see the carved stone bird at Cambridge and was deeply affected by the experience. He took the object away for a time and is said to have risen several times during the night to tangi over it on his dressing table. The Maori king Tawhiao came to pay his respects, as did his fearful side-kick Te Ngakau. All were convinced like the old chieftainess that the object of their veneration had originally come from Hawaiki, that it had become lost, and was now found again. But Te Ngakau

The fighting chief Rewi Manga Maniapoto was convinced the Korotangi was a long-lost treasure of his ancestors. (COURTESY AUCKLAND CITY LIBRARIES)

was afraid. He suggested to Mrs Wilson (Te Aorere) that she throw Korotangi into the Waikato River to avoid suffering the results of any evil which might be worked through it. He seemed convinced that someone like old Rewi was likely to place a makutu on the object to bewitch her. Mrs Wilson paid no heed and when she died soon after it was perhaps natural that some should ascribe her premature death to the spirit world. After all, she was the second person to die in a short time soon after handling the carving.

After this, Major Wilson was anxious to have the Korotangi placed 'where there would be little likelihood of its falling into obnoxious hands', so he considered putting it in a bank vault. He put off doing anything about this and it was his son, Jack, who eventually placed it in the vault of the Bank of New Zealand. When he too died, his widow took the bird away from the bank but 'because of certain happenings' quickly placed it back into safe custody again, this time in the Dominion Museum, a stipulation being that it must never be stored in the dark but should always be exhibited in daylight. Korotangi was acquiring an unsavoury reputation and there were those who whispered that Te Ngakau was right and that the stone bird should have been cast into the Waikato River by John Wilson's wife Te Aorere while the opportunity was there.

For the benefit of the public at large it was suggested in 1881 that casts be made of the Korotangi for display purposes. This idea originated with W. L. Buller, the well-known ornithologist, and it was thanks to his good offices with major Wilson that the carved bird was sent to the noted scientist Julius von Haast, then Director of the Canterbury Museum in Christchurch, whose task it became to produce a number of copies. During 1882 these copies were distributed to the major museums in the country.

As well as being involved with the making of casts of the Korotangi, Julius von Haast was first also to publish an account of the controversial relic, and this appeared in the 1881 edition of the *Transactions and Proceedings of the New Zealand Institute*. The paper had also been read before the Philosophical Society in that year and contained von Haast's comments about aspects of the object's history thus far and scientific opinions on the techniques employed in executing the carving. Essentially, it added no new facts to the growing dossier of speculation and hearsay – with one possible exception. The Premier, Sir George Grey, and the Minister for Native Affairs, John Sheehan, had both seen Korotangi in May 1879, during a visit to the Waikato and were so fascinated that they came away talking about it to anyone who would listen.

There followed in the late 1880s intense debate on all aspects of the Korotangi. But although a lot of people had good intentions, and the opportunity was there to do something about it, not one suggestion seems to have been acted on, and not one promising lead followed up. A few searching questions were asked about the Korotangi's authenticity, about the dubious circumstances of its discovery, about the translations of numerous waiata which referred to lost birds of various kinds, and so on. But to be fair, there simply weren't enough facts to go on. The whole Korotangi edifice had thus far been built only on hearsay and later reminiscences. It is interesting to note in passing that, more than a century later, very little appears to have changed in this respect.

The next significant occurrence in a chronologically based telling of the Korotangi story concerns the noted Maori scholar Edward Tregear. He realised that the only way to get to the bottom of the matter would be to obtain all the missing details 'straight from the horse's mouth'. If anyone knew what was what – apart from Albert Walker, of course, who by now was proving difficult to pin down – the present owner Major Wilson would. So Tregear contacted Wilson and invited him to write a comprehensive paper on the subject which he – Tregear – would present before the Philosophical Society on Wilson's behalf. Wilson agreed but several years elapsed before anything materialised. When it did, Wilson with tongue in cheek commented that he had promised the paper for so long that some people had facetiously been asking 'when the Korotangi would sing'.

At a meeting of the Wellington Philosophical Society on 17 November 1887, Tregear read Wilson's paper at last. Although much was expected, it provided very little new information. The basic problems remained unresolved: Wilson was either unable – or unwilling – to disclose precisely where, when and by whom the Korotangi had been discovered.

Renewed efforts to deal with these questions meant publication of his paper was delayed for two years. Meantime, new problems arose. The need to determine how the Korotangi had come into Walker's possession was the largest difficulty facing members of the Society. W.M. Maskell, Registrar of the University of New Zealand, spoke for all when he stated that Walker should be found and asked to make a clarifying statement. He further claimed that the honour of all the museums in the colony was at stake because all had accepted the Korotangi as genuine and all had displayed models of it. He pointed out also that seeds of doubt had already been sown regarding the authenticity of the Korotangi, and the very integrity of the Society itself was under threat as a result. He was referring to a communication received from a Mr W.E. Gudgeon containing a signed statement from a Maori War veteran, Lt. Col. McDonnell, stating the Korotangi was a fraud perpetuated by Albert Walker upon Major Drummond Hay, who considered himself an expert in Maori curiosities. McDonnell further asserted that Walker told him he had actually brought the carving on board a New Zealand coaster and that Hay had sold it to Wilson for £5. Some of this was true and some wasn't. Hay *didn't* sell Korotangi to Wilson – Walker did. And the purchase price *wasn't* £5 – it was £50. In view of these discrepancies it would seem that little value need be placed on the 'New Zealand coaster' story.

The effect of Gudgeon's communication was to throw the whole Korotangi debate into utter confusion. Tregear got in touch with Major Wilson to find out what his response would be to McDonnell's assertions, but more than 18 months passed before the Major gathered enough documentary evidence to verify everything he had said in this paper. This hadn't been much of any significance, but everyone now was on the defensive and maintaining honour and integrity was beginning to loom larger than resolving the Korotangi debate. Tregear presented material to the Philosophical Society on Wilson's behalf in July 1889, and it had the desired effect so far as Wilson was concerned. Members conceded that he was genuine in his acceptance of the Korotangi as a valid Maori relic but felt, on the other hand, that the evidence produced so far in favour of its alleged antiquity was unsatisfactory.

In November 1889 a new element entered the equation. Author and chronicler of things Maori, John White, had just published his six-volume work *Ancient History of the Maori* and as a result still had in place an extensive network of contacts and informers. Attracted by the Korotangi debate, he put out an all-points request for any suitable information. Within a few months, a Maori from the Waikato area by the name of Pera Kiwi contacted him. He provided a different version of the Korotangi waiata, told a new story to account for the origin of the bird, but, most interesting of all, suggested that the relic had originally been found by a European named 'Neiha' while digging out a well.

White died in 1891 and the Pera Kiwi letter lay unnoticed among his papers until 1929 when the ethnologist Elsdon Best found it again. As co-editor of the *Journal of the Polynesian Society* he responded to Kiwi's information with an article entitled 'Notes on the Korotangi or Stone Bird' (Vol. 38, No. 1) in which he cynically dismissed everything with these words: 'Pera has . . . given us a good sample of the powers of imagination possessed by the Maori. 'Tis thus that folktales come into being . . .' The European 'Neiha', having apparently existed only in Pera Kiwi's imagination, hardly rated a mention – let alone an identification. And this is how things would have been unsatisfactorily left. However, Best sent a copy of his article to amateur historian Mr E. Schnackenberg of the Kawhia district and this brought yet more new information about the Korotangi into the open. Schnackenberg believed in the bird's genuineness and gave Best the local version of the carved bird's origins. He also volunteered the intelligence that a European trader by the name of Nazer – the 'Neiha' of Pera Kiwi's story – had actually dug Korotangi out of a spring. But the information seems not to have been followed up.

It wasn't until 1973 that the next important stage was reached. In that year the Dominion Museum published a paper in which the author, Christine Mackay, sought to take a modern scientific look at the Korotangi saga (*Dominion Museum Records in Ethnology*, Vol. 2, No. 10). The results were inconclusive. The paper was skeptical of Korotangi's genuineness, and of factors such as Neiha, or Nazer, and Schnackenberg's ideas. The universal acceptance by Maori of the relic's validity and importance was glossed over.

In 1976 Pacific scholar Robert Langdon was drawn to the Kawhia area and is on record as saying that the visit 'marked the beginning of a series of discoveries that seemed to unravel the mystery of the Korotangi's presence in New Zealand'. He located an unpublished history of the area compiled by a Mr J.E. Aubin in which was a hand-drawn map with the words 'Korotangi found here' and an arrow pointing to the southern side of Aotea harbour. Another local contact, Mr Robert Turnbull, independently produced a similar map with an arrow pointing to a spot marked 'spring', and another to the home of Mr David Morrison, a farmer who lived nearby. Below the map were the words: 'The spring where Korotangi was found is about 600 metres south of Mr Morrison's home . . .' Later, Turnbull provided Langdon with more details which had been supplied to him by Maori informants J. Apiti and Maui Heu. Apiti's site for Korotangi's discovery was a stream a short distance west of the spring, and the finder a Mr Mason. Heu's location 'was the same spring or swamp that Pera Kiwi, Schnackenberg and others had referred to . . .' On a subsequent visit to Mr Morrison, Langdon learned that he, Morrison, had always understood that Korotangi had been found in the 'Hawaiki' swamp on his property – a piece of news which Mr Langdon invested with a great deal of significance. At the Land Transfer Office in Hamilton he was able to verify from records that 'Hawaiki' was indeed a place name which applied to an extremely narrow corridor of land following the course of a stream between Kawhia and Aotea. Was this Hawaiki the same Hawaiki mentioned in numerous pieces of Maori folklore as the source of the Korotangi?

Various people to whom the discovery of the Korotangi has been ascribed over the years – especially Mason and Nazer – had been landowners in the Kawhia/Aotea area in days gone by and this fact may have spawned some of the stories linking them both with the unearthing of the sacred carved bird.

The matter of the Korotangi can be seen as a series of seven unsolved mysteries . . .

The Mystery of Korotangi's Execution

How was the object made? How does the carving technique compare with other Maori artefacts of culture or war? In 1887 Edward Tregear called it 'a beautiful work of art'. But was it a beautiful *Maori* work of art? Or a beautiful

European work of art? Even after studying all the clues available it is still not easy to decide. Neither can we be quite sure just *how* it was made.

In a paper written for the Dominion Museum in 1973 Christine Mackay said:

> It is a detailed, naturalistic carving of a perched bird, with pigeon-like plumage . . . The blunt feathered feet are, however, more reminiscent of an owl, and the plumage of neat regularised feathers is non-specific. It is in fact a representation of no particular species, but rather an imaginary conglomeration with the attributes of several birds . . . The artistic features of Korotangi are clearly unusual in the context of Maori art.

In summing up, she added:

> It is difficult to believe that Korotangi in any way belongs to an art form ancestral to that of the classic Maori. Technological aspects of the bird similarly cast doubt upon its assumed Polynesian origin. ('Korotangi – An Enigmatic Stone Bird', *Dominion Museum Records in Ethnology*, Vol. 2, No. 10.)

In 1929 the editors of the *Journal of the Polynesian Society* had expressed similar sentiments. This assessment was by no means new. At first glance it seemed obvious that the Korotangi was neither a Maori nor a Polynesian item. As far back as 1881 Professor Julius von Haast had written that it was 'carved in a bold and careful way . . . with a sharp implement, either of iron or bronze, of which, as we know, the Maori had no knowledge. The lines are all cut so evenly that it could not have been done with a stone implement.'

A point which is often overlooked is that hiding away in its base is a hole 10 mm in diameter and 55 mm deep. It appears to have been made at some unknown date for a mounting peg, or similar. Christine Mackay says of it that it is 'undoubtedly the work of a mechanical steel drill'. If this is the case, the hole becomes just one more mysterious element in a pot-pourri of mysterious elements.

It seems clear that the long-lost heirloom brought from Hawaiki was not made by Maori at all. Somehow they must have acquired it from another culture.

The Mystery of the Material Used

To date no one has been able to pinpoint exactly where the dark green serpentine rock used to carve the strange stone bird came from. In 1889, at a meeting of the Wellington Philosophical Society, Mr Edward Tregear claimed that 'one geologist stated that the stone of which the bird was composed was the pipe-stone of the North American Indian'. No elaboration was given and it is difficult for us today to nominate who exactly Mr Tregear's 'geologist' was. The block of stone from which the Korotangi was carved could have come from any one of a dozen different countries; it may never be possible to determine which one. The rock is found in New Zealand, New Guinea, New Caledonia, Australia and North and South America – but in none of the Central or Eastern Pacific islands generally considered to have comprised the immediate ancestral area of the Maori.

The Mystery of Korotangi's Origin

A look at where Korotangi originally came from really needs to start with where 19th-century Maori said it came from – Hawaiki. It was their unshakable belief that it came from the ancestral homeland in the *Tainui* canoe, which, after making landfall on Auckland's east coast, was dragged over the Tamaki portage into the Manukau and thence to Aotea between Kawhia and Raglan. If it is true that Korotangi did make such an epic journey, no wonder its rediscovery in the 1870s was greeted with such excitement. No wonder that, even as late as 1946, the Maori princess Te Puea Herangi said during a visit to see it at the Dominion Museum: 'Please accept my gratitude for permitting me to see and hold this great treasure of my ancestors . . .'

Maori had never doubted that the reappearance of Korotangi was something of a cultural event, and more – that the object itself had once been a sacred emblem, an oracle in time of war, and an ancient atua.

From the pakeha point of view the Korotangi and its alleged antiquity and associations was not such a clear-cut matter. Learned and not so learned men vied with one another to provide some sort of explanation for its origin. Edward Tregear waxed most lyrical:

If this stone carving is a representation of the bird of Chaldean and Hebrew flood-tradition, it is probably of immense antiquity (perhaps brought even from the very source of Deluge-stories in far-off Asia): it may be quite the oldest relic of primitive man and their beliefs now in existence.

Julius von Haast tried a different tack. He exhibited an ancient Japanese bronze figure cast in the shape of a bird 'the character of which is in many respects not unlike the specimen carved from stone' (the Korotangi). 'To my mind,' he continued, 'there is no doubt that both have a somewhat similar origin.' Some members of the Wellington Philosophical Society were a little cagey about the whole Korotangi affair. A few were even cynical. Mr Coleman Phillips said that 'if the bird had really been brought over in the Tainui canoe, as alleged, similar carvings should be found in some of the South Sea islands whence the Tainui came . . .', insinuating quietly that such was not the case. Major Gudgeon asserted that if 'the Korotangi was a bona fide Maori relic of ancient times, the tribe to whom it formerly belonged would have exact traditions of it'. On the face of it – they did. In the *Journal of the Polynesian Society* (Vol. 38, No. 1, 1929) the editors said: 'the Maori folk claimed it [Korotangi] as an old heirloom of the Tainui people, and so we are told it was brought from Hawaiki, the former home of the Maori, by their ancestors.' Others didn't rule out any possibility at all to account for Korotangi being in New Zealand. Mr W.M. Maskell, registrar of the University of New Zealand, said in 1889: 'it seemed not impossible that the bird might be accounted for in another way . . .' This 'way' is, of course, closely allied with the principal purpose of this book: the determination of whether Europeans or Asiatics could have been in New Zealand before Cook in 1769. Maskell was wondering whether any such surreptitious visitors could have brought the stone bird here with them (Minutes of a meeting of the Wellington Philosophical Society, 31 July 1989, as recorded in 'Transactions of the New Zealand Institute', Vol. 22).

From the date when Vasco de Gama rounded the Cape of Good Hope to the arrival of Captain Cook in New Zealand, somewhere near 350 years elapsed. During that period the eastern and southern seas were traversed by hundreds of ships – Portuguese, French, Spanish, Dutch and English . . . As regarded the Portuguese and the Dutch . . . the captains of their early ships were not allowed, except in special cases like Tasman's, to publish records of their voyages. These records were sent in only to their respective Governments, and . . . in the archives of Lisbon and Amsterdam there might be found numbers of such unpublished 'ships' logs'. In the 350 years just mentioned there was room for any number of ships to have touched at New Zealand . . .

Maskell went on to make the point that from any one of these vessels the stone bird might have been stolen 'and afterwards, made the subject of songs, of legends, and all sorts or rubbish'. He moved that the Council of the Society:

> . . . open communication with the Governments of Portugal and Holland, with a view to ascertaining whether there are to be found in the archives of these countries any records of ships which may have touched at New Zealand before the visit of Captain Cook, besides those of the expedition of Tasman. (ibid)

Edward Tregear considered this the most productive of all the lines of enquiry proposed so far to get to the bottom of the Korotangi mystery. Yet although Maskell's resolution was carried, no subsequent progress seems to have taken place, and the opportunity of procuring what was called at the time 'inform-ation of a valuable character in a geographical sense' looks as though it just slipped away.

In 1961, a variation of the 'pre-Cook-vessel-in-New-Zealand' theme was put forward by writer Barry Mitcalfe. 'The Korotangi is certainly Eastern in the style of its carving,' he said, and quoted W.J. Phillips on similar birds having been found in Malaya, Japan, and in the 'excavations at Ur on the Chaldees'. He continued:

> Possibly the Korotangi came from the wreck of a Tamil (Southern Indian) vessel [dealt with elsewhere in this book] which may have come ashore between Kawhia and Raglan on the West Coast. In 1877, shifting sands revealed the ribs of a vessel, supposedly Asiatic in origin . . . Until the remains are again revealed and then, if possible radio-carbon tested, we will

have to rely on other evidence for the origin of the Korotangi. ('Korotangi, The Sacred Bird', *Te Ao Hou*, No. 37, December 1961.)

So the evidence for the Korotangi being a genuine and long-lost treasure of the Maori, and the evidence for it being a more mundane and recently executed object, is very evenly poised indeed.

The Mystery of the Waiatas

The Maori case for the Korotangi being a long-lost treasure of their ancestors rests rather more heavily on a series of ancient songs, or rather, what is essentially a number of different versions of the same song. Soon after its discovery, and while it was on display in Cambridge, an unnamed chieftainess wept tears over the relic and sang a song whose words King Tawhiao's aide, Te Ngakau, later gave to one-time owner, Major Wilson. Mr C.O. Davis, the 'well-known native scholar', provided the English translation. The most significant words in the song for us are:

> Let us gaze upon the feathers carved
> *In lands remote . . .*

It is this statement in all its various versions which is held up as proof that the songs are about a *carved image* (i.e. the Korotangi itself), rather than a real bird. Wilson and Tregear provide a slightly different translation of Te Ngakau's words which brings the point out with even greater clarity. The Maori words are:

> Ehara tena he manu Maori waiho,
> Me titiro ki te huruhuru whakairoiro mai,
> No tawhiti . . .

> And the English translation:
> This is not a Maori bird.
> Consider – look at the carved feathers thereof.
> It (evidently) comes from a distance –
> A foreign country, or over the sea.

Even more intriguing is that 19 years before Korotangi was found Sir George Grey had a Korotangi poem in his 1853 *Poems, Traditions and Chaunts of the Maoris*. Significantly, it contained the following words as translated by Archdeacon Maunsell:

> Stop! We must look at the feathers
> Brought here, carried from a distance . . .

In 1929, the editors of the *Journal of Polynesian Society* (Vol. 38) appeared to be bordering on the cynical when they stated that the talk of 'carved feathers' appeared to have been the result of a desire to connect the songs with the stone bird. They said 'it is clear that the songs refer to a living bird, and *not* the Korotangi, and that previous translations which appeared to tie the songs to the bird were strained productions' – notwithstanding the fact that the translators involved were nationally known for their integrity and skill. These comments were probably only one person's opinion, of course, and against that we can stack the many different songs which *do* mention carved feathers.

A complicating factor in the issue of the Korotangi waiata is that numerous folklore stories around the country deal with a *real* pet bird and the owner's grief when it became lost. The most common version usually concerns a fisher capturing a duck and keeping it as a pet. During his absence his wife ill-treats the bird and it escapes so the fisher composes a lament. In some versions of this he gets back a few of its feathers. In others, the bird dies in a swamp or stream and turns to stone. No wonder the discovery of the stone Korotangi caused such a stir! It's a question of what you choose to believe. The ancient 'lost bird' waiata either refer to the Korotangi – or they don't.

The Mystery of Korotangi's Discovery

Even the circumstances of Korotangi's discovery in the 1870s have become distorted and shrouded in mystery. No one has yet determined exactly *who* found it, *where*, or *when*. The only information we have is that 'some time between 1872 and 1879' the relic was found by 'members of a native tribe' in the roots of a large manuka tree which had just been blown down by high winds 'somewhere between Kawhia and Raglan'. There is even doubt about this particular scenario. If, as Christine Mackay asserts, the object was in Maori possession before the period of European contact, and there is no satisfactory traditional evidence to support this (providing of course you ignore top-level Maori assertions to the contrary, and dismiss all Korotangi songs and folktales out of hand), an unrecorded ship's visit or shipwreck is another possible origin and the 'found-in-the-roots-of-a-tree' story might just be that – a story. Mackay echoes others when she further states that the Korotangi could possibly have been brought to New Zealand in the very early days of European contact, or made here at that time, with European tools. Even under such conditions 'it could still have been precious, been lost or hidden, and found again'.

Her 'most plausible conjecture' is that the bird arrived or was made in New Zealand some time last century, 'even immediately prior to its discovery', principally because 'the circumstances of its alleged finding in the roots of a blown down tree have no contemporary description or documentation'.

Notwithstanding such scepticism, it is known that the first European owner of the Korotangi, Albert Walker, had a Maori wife whose connections with the 'native tribe' who found the object have never been fully explored. The inference from the few sketchy details available is that the original finders did not appreciate the significance of their find until Walker received a reaction from Major Drummond Hay in Cambridge, which he communicated back to his wife, who in turn told the tribe, and from whence the whole thing began to snowball. The fact that Walker later claimed to have obtained the relic from on board a New Zealand coaster is puzzling, and either speaks of the state of his mental health or else his partiality to spirituous liquors – or both. There is some significance in the fact that soon after news of Korotangi's discovery broke, and after Walker had rightly or wrongly pocketed the sum of £50 for it from Major Wilson, he left the country and was last heard of 'roaming about the South Seas', well out of the way of awkward questions.

So it seems the best chance ever of ascertaining the real details of Korotangi's discovery probably went to oblivion with Albert Walker and expired with him at the time of his death. He alone knew what was what, and recognising this, members of the Wellington Philosophical Society spent long hours in the late 1880s trying to track him down and generally debating how to resolve the whole issue. Of course they never did, and more than 100 years later we are no closer to a solution either – unless, of course, there is anything to the story that the Korotangi was found on a Mr Morrison's property in a swampy area of ground known as 'Hawaiki' which is situated between the Kawhia and Aotea Harbours. After all, the local Maori people had insisted all along that the object of their veneration had come from a place called Hawaiki.

The Mystery of Korotangi's Significance

Why would the old-time Maori people have wanted a stone bird? Was it for use, or ornament? Scattered throughout the written record are brief attempts to address these questions.

Major Wilson, who once owned the Korotangi, wrote that in the migrations Maori 'doubtless brought all they could with them of their "household gods"'. C.O. Davis, the Maori translator, also said that 'if tradition is to be relied on, each vessel of the fleet brought to these shores some lasting monuments of ancient art'. If we can concede, therefore, that the Korotangi qualifies as 'ancient art', or a 'household god', it doesn't become too difficult to appreciate why it was accepted for inclusion in the 'baggage' of a migrating canoe such as the Tainui.

But what was the Korotangi for? We read that it was a sacred object, that it was highly venerated, that copious tears were shed in its presence, and that ancient songs were wailed over it. We have been told that in ancient times it may have been used as a talisman, or oracle, to be consulted in time of war. It was tapu. It had spiritual significance. It could be a channel for evil.

Possibly the most credible explanation for Korotangi's purpose and significance is to be found hidden in the writings of Sir Maui Pomare (*Legends of the Maori*, 1934):

> After the Tainui canoe had been dragged across the Tamaki portage to the west coast it sailed south. The high priest Rakataura did not remain with

the canoe, but went exploring southward with some of the crew and his sister Hiaora. At Karioi he set up his tuahu, named Tuahu Papa. Rakataura travelled along and built an altar at Heahea. This placed was named Ahurei afer a temple in Tahiti. He met Hoturoa on a beach between Moeatoa and Tirua and the two chiefs were reconciled. Hoturoa gave his sister Kahurere to Rakataura as his wife. Hoturoa hauled his canoe ashore at a place called Maketu and the priests each set up a white stone, one at the bow and one at the stern of the canoe. They are about 60 feet apart. The inland stone was set up to represent Hani, war and death at the bow; the one nearer the shore was Puna, representing peace and growth of mankind whakatupu tangata.

Rakataura's great work was the exploration of the forests of the King Country and the distribution of the sacred emblems of fertility which he had brought from Hawaiki to plant in the new land. These were mauri kohatu, or talismanic stone emblems, particularly intended to ensure a permanent abundance of forest birds for food. The bird kohatu was called also mauri manu and whatu ahuru manu. They were small stones, probably carved, which had been charmed by the high priest in Tahiti before the departure of the Tainui.

Rakataura and wife travelled inland, set up tuahu and named places after themselves in order to establish land rights. The tohunga had a number of followers, and several of these men he sent out with these stone mascots with directions where to leave the mauri. Hotu and Hiaora left several mauri on the mountains from Hakarimata to Pirongia southward. Hotu settled at a place called Paewhenua, in the upper Waipa valley where there were birds in abundance. At Paewhenua, where Hotu settled, there was a large mangeo tree, and in this the descendants of Hotu preserved the sacred stone . . .

After reading this we could almost bring ourselves to agree that the Korotangi may well have been a 'mauri kohatu', or talismanic stone emblem.

Priceless Relic . . . or Hoax?

The simplest way to account for the puzzling elements and discrepancies surrounding the Korotangi may be that it is a hoax. Maori people as a whole are horrified by the suggestion of any such thing, but the possibility has been raised many times.

The first seeds of doubt were planted in 1887 when a letter from Lt. Col. McDonnell was presented by Gudgeon to a meeting of the Wellington Philosophical Society. In it McDonnell stated that the carved bird was a fraud perpetuated by Albert Walker upon Major Drummond Hay in Cambridge. Why he should say such a thing is a mystery on its own. McDonnell might have had it in for Walker for one reason or another and may have considered this to be a perfect way of discrediting him. Who knows? But because very little detail accompanied the letter those involved with the saga were sent into an immediate panic. Mr Maskell said the matter would have to be settled quickly because it affected the honour of the societies affiliated to the New Zealand Institute. Also, most museums in the country were displaying a model of the relic, and if the whole thing was a fraud they and the societies would end up with much egg on their faces. The best way for the question to be cleared up would be to communicate with Albert Walker and ask him to make a definite statement on the matter. S. Percy Smith agreed, and outlined other ways the Korotangi could be verified as a genuine Maori relic too. But for all the talk, nothing was done and we seem to be left, as the Dominion Museum's Christine Mackay puts it:

> . . . with Albert Walker as prime suspect in the perpetration of a hoax. Perhaps, as Mr Phillips suggested during the Society's debate on the matter, hoax is too strong a word, and what started out as a joke or trick went further than intended. If he did indeed purchase the bird off a ship, perhaps Walker showed it to Major Drummond Hay as merely a curiosity, and the unpredicted and excited reception it received from Maori leaders led to the idea of financial benefits to be gained from perpetrating the deception. Why, if Walker was embroiled in a hoax, he ever mentioned purchasing the bird from a coastal ship, is puzzling, and even more tantalising is the question why this apparently plausible explanation was cast aside by observers at the time. (*Dominion Museum Records in Ethnology*, Vol. 2, No. 10.)

Fact or Fiction?

The whole Korotangi investigation was badly bungled by all concerned in the 1880s and it is now impossible to sort out fact from fiction. Recently, efforts have been made to identify the ultimate source of the Korotangi by seeking help from the various museums around the world. Directors in the 21 countries approached thus far, however, have not been able to help simply because they were unable to find comparative material in their respective collections. The countries approached are Canada, Egypt, England, France, Holland, Hong Kong, India, Israel, Japan, Korea, Malaysia, Mexico, Peru, Philippines, Singapore, South Africa, Sri Lanka, Taiwan, Turkey, USA and Vietnam. It might be a good idea to continue this line of enquiry. The two famous English antique dealers, Sothebys and Christies, are unable to recall items similar to the Korotangi passing through their rooms, but there are many other auction houses around the world which would be worth approaching.

Meantime, we have four options. We can take the view just as the Maori people do that the stone bird was brought to New Zealand by migrants from the Pacific many centuries ago and then lost or purposely hidden. We can believe that in an effort to give material form to old traditions about a lost pet bird, and the songs concerning it, Maori declared Korotangi upon discovery to actually *be* that missing bird. We might like to think that the object was part of the cargo of some early ship which visited our shores – before *or* after Cook – and which subsequently may have been wrecked, or stolen from. Finally, we might be convinced that the whole thing was an elaborate hoax designed to get one back on some 19th-century, pompous, self-styled expert on things Maori, and that the bird may actually have been carved by some early sealer or whaler with time on his hands at sea.

You decide.

7

The Mystery Wreck of Ruapuke Beach

Appearances and Reappearances:
The Ancient Wreck

There have been many shipwrecks on New Zealand coasts over the years. Since the first one, recorded in 1795, there have been a staggering 2100. This does not include small pleasure craft, or any trawlers and suchlike under 9 metres in length, but only those larger vessels more commonly thought of as 'sea-going'. On top of this 2100 are a further dozen or so officially described as 'unidentified'. Another 10 or 12, also unidentified, are suspected of dating back to prehistoric times. So if unknown Europeans (or others) *were* in New Zealand before 1769 the wrecks of their ships should be the best supporting evidence of the fact . . . or should they?

In the *Raglan County Chronicle* of 10 January 1903, a few paragraphs featured details of an old wreck on a nearby beach which a local Maori claimed he 'could remember for 80 years', and which his grandfather had told him was there 'long before Captain Cook's arrival'. Ever since the article appeared, speculation on the wreck – *and* items found in the vicinity – has run riot and common sense seems to have been absent.

According to the *Chronicle* article:

Mr Kennedy, builder of Auckland, today visited Raglan and is so much interested in the old wreck on the Aotea beach that he is desirous of organising a syndicate to unearth it and ascertain its value . . . No 'treasure trove' has ever been obtained from it. It is probable the wreck came there *before the Maori's advent in New Zealand* [emphasis in original] so that it is likely to prove very interesting, if not valuable.

It is proposed that a Raglan committee be formed and that Mr Cheeseman, curator of the Auckland Museum, be interviewed with the object of getting him to take charge of an exploration picnic at Easter.

Some years ago Mr T.B. Hill procured a piece of the wreck and found it to be teak: it was so well preserved that he had it turned in the shape of a ruler, as a souvenir of a pleasant picnic, and Messrs Phillips and Liddell cut out a large kit of bolts which are supposed to consist of a mixture of copper and iron.

A surveyor, a friend of Mr Kennedy, took the bearings many years ago so that there should be no difficulty in locating it.

It is surmised that the bell with the Tamil inscription, now in the Auckland Museum, came from this ship.

Who would have thought that right here in New Zealand was the wreck of a large ship which was here long before Captain Cook's arrival and possibly even 'before the Maori's advent in New Zealand'? What more could historical researchers ask for? Here was a wreck of obvious antiquity within easy reach and still, apparently, with its ancient cargo intact. It was just the kind of proof required to demonstrate a pre-1769, non-Polynesian presence in New Zealand. There could be nothing better for the purpose. Quite likely it was the country's most important archaeological and historical find yet, and on the face of it, certainly had the potential to answer questions about contact from outside the Pacific region in earlier centuries. So how did Mr Kennedy's 'exploration picnic' get on? What relics were discovered, what new information brought to light, and what conclusions were reached by Mr Cheeseman?

The answer to these questions is . . . very little indeed.

Mr Kennedy's picnic, and all subsequent attempts to find out more about this particular wreck, resolved nothing. It remains unidentified. In an age which can produce Scud-busting Patriot missiles, 'smart' bombs and surveillance satellites, no one, it seems, can identify a few old planks of wood held together by an assortment of copper and brass hardware. So is the wreck of Tamil origin – as hinted at in the *Chronicle* article – or isn't it?

Two factors need to be considered first. Was Mr Hill the discoverer of the wreck? And is teak a significant timber for a New Zealand-found wreck to be constructed of?

Mr T.B. Hill was a one-time chemist of Queen Street, Auckland, who gave up pharmacy to move south and settle on a farm in the Ruapuke/Raglan area. Together with a friend, Mr R.J. O'Sullivan, an inspector of schools, the pair conducted an examination of the wreckage in 1875 as it then lay exposed in the bed of the Toreparu River, which flows into the ocean midway between Aotea and Raglan Harbours. Local historian Mr E.H. Schnackenberg describes (Hunt, 1955) what happened on that day:

> They found the portion of the deck and sides of a large vessel, constructed, it is said, entirely of teak, built with three skins, on the diagonal principle, the planking being fastened together with wooden screws, or tree-nails, and strengthened with brass bolts. No metal nails had been employed in its construction, while the heavy beams and timbers were secured with large brass bolts of unusually good quality measuring 2 feet, 10½ inches (87.7 cm) long and each weighing nearly 14 pounds (6.35 kg) . . .

The two men found that the ship's bell had been removed from its position, and just below where it should have been was a bronze plate inscribed with what they believed to be Tamil characters, 'of which language both were ignorant', the record tells us. For the moment, though, the origin of the script was immaterial. Here was a piece of tangible evidence with the potential to prove a pre-Cook non-Polynesian presence in New Zealand and Messrs Hill and O'Sullivan seemed to appreciate this fact. Mr Hill prised the plate from the decking, packed it in a box, and sent it to Raglan for trans-shipment on to Auckland to be preserved, and for the script to be deciphered. But, somehow, the priceless plate vanished without trace en route and was never seen again.

The 1870s was the era of the big-time souvenir hunters where almost any relic of a bygone age was fair game. In the absence of any laws to prevent such a practice, there was heavy traffic in all types of New Zealand antiquities at this time not only to wealthy individuals all over Europe, but to museums and other institutions as well. These facts may explain what might have become of the plate. But if such was the case, the object would more than likely have surfaced by now and the fact that it hasn't lends weight to yet another hypothesis, popular in collecting circles for some years, that the plate eventually found its way into the hands of William Colenso, who owned the other half of the puzzle, the so-called 'Tamil' bell – of which more later. When Colenso died, so the story goes, his maid threw out the bulk of her late employer's effects including objects he had acquired over the years, plus an unknown quantity of papers, and the like, and discarded the whole lot down the deep well on their Napier property. There is an outside chance the missing plate may have featured in this thoughtless 1899 incident.

But back to the wreck. Sometimes Hill and O'Sullivan have been referred to as the discoverers, but this is not strictly correct. The reference in a book *Memories of an Early Settler* (1929), containing the reminiscences of one William Duncan, who with his parents settled in the area in 1864, would seem to indicate that long before Hill's 1875 examination the wreck was known of.

A feature of considerable interest to visitors was the remains of the wreckage of a vessel which lay nearby covered with sand at the mouth of the Toreparu River, where the Horokawau and other streams enter the sea. The vessel was some distance from the high tidal mark, and no true conjecture has ever been supplied how the vessel was wrecked or to what nation she belonged. None of the Maoris living have any recollection how she got there . . .

Of course, the last statement needs to be considered in the light of the fact that about 1819 the local tribe had largely been driven out of their home territory by Waikato people, and while it was difficult to find anyone who knew anything about local history, it was not impossible. As mentioned earlier, one old man could remember the wreck for the previous 80 years, and his grandfather had told him it was there 'long before Captain Cook's arrival'.

One of the chief factors which has caused the wreck to maintain a continuing air of mystery over the years has been that, almost constantly, its exact whereabouts has been concealed by sand. Only four or five times in a century will a combination of excessive rain and swollen streams scour enough material away to expose it to view again. Apart from the 1875 showing when Hill examined it, and one a decade earlier which William Duncan witnessed, the wreck has been on view in 1890, 1893, 1902, 1912–1914, possibly 1919 and, apparently, not since. But each time it *has* been exposed, it has been the object of varying degrees of attention and study, as well as presenting locals with yet another opportunity to remove souvenirs from it. Pieces of teak and a bronze name plate were taken in 1875, and, in 1890, a number of brass bolts and wooden tree-nails were taken. On one later occasion, someone even tried blasting timber from the wreck for farm construction purposes.

Mr E.H. Schnackenberg wrote (Hunt, 1955) about the cause of the wreck's periodic appearances and his comments will eventually become relevant to our study.

> . . . the vessel lies, submerged by sand, to the north of the effluence of the river Toreparu, which received its waters from a swamp of several hundred acres. In 1914 an exceptional deluge of rain was responsible for a high flood, which according to an eyewitness (Mr F.E. Trolov) rose to such a level that the swamp resembled an inland lake. For a distance of two miles, a channel was torn through the whole length of the swamp and immense quantities of raupo and other vegetation were carried seawards to be deposited where the river met the rollers. Thousands of tons of sand were also carried by the torrent, and, caught by the vegetation, formed an impervious dam about a mile long and many chains wide to the southward of the river mouth. The floodwaters were thereby forced to seek another outlet, and quickly swept away the same on the northern beach, exposing the wreck mid-channel.

Ancient Wreck and Ancient Relic:
The Tamil Bell

When Hill in 1875 reported that the 'ship's bell had been removed from its position' on the wreck it's difficult to determine just what exactly he was basing this observation on. Was he making a wild guess? Was he conversant with the layout of older-style ocean-going ships and therefore knew exactly where the ship's bell ought to be? Could it be that he was so familiar with Colenso's bell he was letting himself be influenced by it and the characters inscribed on it? Especially after discovering a bronze plate attached to the deck, featuring as it did what he believed to be a Tamil-like script similar to that on the bell. This latter fact is probably what caused him to jump to the conclusion that since the lettering on both the plate and the bell seemed identical to him it automatically followed that he had been dealing all along with the wreck of a Tamil ship. In which assumption he may have been right, or he may have been wrong. We still don't know. Whatever the case, the Ruapuke wreck has been popularly referred to since as the 'Tamil' wreck, and because Colenso's bell is largely responsible for this it needs to be looked at closely in order to better understand the wreck itself.

There are various conflicting accounts of where the bell was found. Major Wilson, one-time owner of the Korotangi, another relic which has caused a lot of headaches, says that the bell was discovered 'in the interior of the North Island' by Colenso in 1836. This echoes what Colenso had to say. Bequeathing the item to the then Colonial Museum, he sent a note in his own handwriting saying:

> This antique bell was found by the Exhibitor in the interior of the North Island in 1836. The inscription is believed to be Javanese. It has been sent to England for translation. W.C.

Colenso's reference here to finding the bell in the 'interior of the North Island' has caused confusion over the years. A number have jumped to the conclusion that he was referring to the Taupo area, because Taupo is about as 'interior' as you can possibly get.

But other people, and the facts, would seem to contradict this idea. Colenso does not seem to have been anywhere near Taupo in 1836. In 1834 he took up a position at the Bay of Islands as a missionary-printer for the London-based Church Missionary Society. To his annoyance he found the equipment he was meant to work with was less than satisfactory. As researcher C.G. Hunt (1955) put it:

> . . . for seven years he laboured at his task in spite of great difficulties, and it is extremely unlikely that he ever left the Bay of Islands district for more than a few days at a time during this period. He certainly could not have left to undertake a journey to Taupo which, in those days, would have involved months of travel by canoe and on foot. ('Some notes on the mystery wreck on Ruapuke Beach for the Waikato Scientific Association')

So where *was* the bell found? When Colenso referred to the interior of the North Island, he was using the word 'interior' in its broadest sense. To him the words 'inland' and 'interior' seem to have been interchangeable. Any place several kilometres away from the sea became his 'interior' – no matter which part of the North Island he may for the time being have been referring to.

The correct version of how and where the bell was found is as follows: Colenso was on a small expedition in the Whangarei area in 1836 when he came upon a party of Maori cooking food out in the open in what appeared to be a small pot. A.G. Bagnall and G.C. Peterson in their book *William Colenso* (1948) go on to say:

The inscriptions around the side of the 'Tamil Bell' have caused a number of people to link it with the wreck of a 'Tamil' ship under the sands of Ruapuke Beach. It is estimated to be up to 500 years old. (COLLECTION OF THE MUSEUM OF NEW ZEALAND TE PAPA TONGAREWA, NEG. NO. B 011109)

. . . apart from a few utensils they might have obtained from pakehas scattered around the coast, the natives, being a neolithic people, did not possess fire-resisting cooking utensils, and Colenso's interest was aroused. He examined the article to find to his surprise that it was a bronze bell with the rim broken off. The natives are said to have informed him that it had belonged to the tribe for many generations, but its immediate owners had found it when a large tree had been blown down and it was left exposed to view. Colenso's interest was intensified by the discovery that around the upper band of the bell was what appeared to be an inscription in some oriental script. He secured the bell and this ancient relic, indicating the possibility of the visit to New Zealand of an Asiatic vessel long before Tasman's discovery, has ever since provided historians with a puzzle that still remains unsolved.

In support of the idea that the bell was found in the North Auckland region by Colenso rather than the Taupo area, an intriguing little piece of Tainui tradition handed down by the Kawhia/Raglan people would appear to explain all if accepted at face value. According to them, a bell had been in the possession of a section of the tribe until it was taken from them by a raiding party who later returned to North Auckland with it long before the 1836 rediscovery. The scene of the loss, and the apparent home of the object up until that time, was a small settlement by the name of 'Te Pahu', which, rather significantly, just happens to mean 'the bell'.

Colenso was supposed to have written a 'long and interesting' history of the Tamil bell which no one has ever been able to find. The feeling is that it went the way of many of his other writings which have been irretrievably lost or destroyed. Sadly, his maid and the family well at Napier may have more to answer for than first thought.

In 1865 Colenso exhibited the bell at the New Zealand Exhibition and some information in the Jurors' Reports of that event clearly shows that even at this stage the relic was being endowed with Tamil associations. It was stated rather ungrammatically in the Reports to have been 'found by the exhibitor in the interior of the North Island in 1837, on which is an inscription in Tamil . . .'.

A Mr J.T. Thompson appears to have taken the first steps towards having the inscription translated. He is said to have first viewed the bell at the Exhibition, to have had it photographed, and copies sent off to various parts of India to help determine its origin. In Southern India, the Tamil people immediately recognised it as the upper part of a ship's bell of a kind commonly in former use among them. The embossed inscription was stated to be in an obsolete style which made use of characters of a bygone era. These were translated as meaning 'Mohoyideen Buks – ship's bell'.

The bell itself was inspected in the Dominion Museum in 1926 by the Bishop of Dornakal, South India, and it was his opinion that it was not an object of particularly great antiquity. In 1941 a third examination was carried out, this time by Mr J.M. Barron, a scholar from Straits Settlements, who considered the translation should more correctly be 'the bell of Mukaiyathan's ship'. Soon after, a Tamil scholar by the name of Professor Visvanathan estimated the bell's age at between 400 and 500 years old and said that, in his opinion, it had originally belonged to a seafaring branch of the Tamil race known as the Marakkaiyar, who earlier has settled in Java and surrounding islands, and who, having formerly been Hindu, had later converted to Islam. As a result, it was entirely possible that the bell may not have come from India at all.

Researcher C.G. Hunt (1955) continues our study with some relevant observations on how the bell might have entered New Zealand.

However intriguing the story of the discovery may be, the main interest of the relic is in its age and the manner in which it reached New Zealand. It being established from the inscription that the bell is of considerable age, even if it does not possess 'great antiquity', and neglecting for the moment the possibility of its having been brought to New Zealand in an early whaling ship, it could have reached these shores only in the vessel to which it belonged or in a canoe of a Polynesian sea rover. The Tamils are known to have made voyages to Malaya, where traces of Indian culture are to be found today, and there is a possibility that some venturesome trader entered the Pacific, where the bell could have come into the possession of the neolithic Polynesians, to whom it would have been a treasure worthy of being carried with them on their sea wanderings . . .

The alternative possibility, heightened by the discovery in 1877 of the wreck of a supposed Asiatic vessel buried in the sands of the west coast of the Auckland province near Raglan, is that the bell was taken by the natives from some ancient ship that reached these shores only to meet disaster, possibly in the fifteenth or sixteenth century, long before the advent of Tasman.

(For a more in-depth look at the possible origins of this bell see Brett Hilder's article in the *Journal of the Polynesian Society*, Vol. 84, No. 4.)

The Search for Complementary Evidence

When the inscription on the bell was deciphered, and its Tamil associations finally verified, William Colenso considered the mystery of the Ruapuke wreck solved. So far as he was concerned, the bell *must* have come from the wreck. And since such an item could only have come from a Tamil ship – or the wreckage of one – and since no one at the time seemed able to furnish a better explanation, the link between mystery relic and mystery wreck became cemented in place in the public mind – and has remained that way.

As soon as this linkage was established, there took place a general casting about for other relics capable of being ascribed to the ship at Ruapuke. Professional and amateur alike had a field day. Any unidentified object, or anything difficult to explain within 100 kilometres of the wreck site, either came from it, or was wrought by possible survivors from it. Almost nothing was safe – as the following list of items sometimes mentioned in the same breath as the Ruapuke wreck demonstrates: the discovery of 17th-century bottles and a skeleton in a suit of armour dug up in the Taranaki area, the discovery of a number of man-sized stoneware urns in the interior of a hill near Hamilton, the Korotangi, a steatite figurine found in sub-soil at Mauku, ancient stonework in the area, two uncharacteristic limestone slab pillars found erected near the wreck site, some unusually 'tattooed' rocks at a spot between Whale Bay and Raglan Heads – and so on.

However, the link of any of this material to the wreck is very tenuous indeed and does not merit further consideration here.

Primary Evidence: Relics from the Wreck

The most important relic known to have been taken from the wreck site would have to be the bronze plate featuring a Tamil-like script which Mr T.B. Hill prised from the ship's deck in 1875. Since then, a great variety of other material has been taken as well. Up to 1955 Mr C.G. Hunt spent considerable time tracking down various people known to have acquired items from the site over the years and then tried to have it all properly identified and dated. Thanks largely to his efforts, the mystery wreck of Ruapuke Beach is not now quite the mystery it once was.

An official of the Auckland Institute and Museum visited the wreck site in October 1892. His report is probably the most authoritative 19th-century account in existence of what was actually there at that time. The purpose of the visit was to study the methods and materials used in building the ship with the view to identifying it. An extract from this report will show how detailed the examination was:

[There was only a] portion of wreck visible when I visited the place and I had no means of ascertaining how much was covered in the sand. The superficial area was 55 to 60 square feet, the surface flat and composed of planks generally 9 inches, with a few 6 inches, wide. This deck, or whatever it may be, is composed of 5 planks in depth, each plank nominally 2 inches thick, giving a total of 10 inches in thickness. The timber is like inferior pine with many knots but though discoloured and somewhat dozed is in a fair state of preservation . . . But the construction is remarkable, each layer of planking being at an angle of 45° from the last layer; the top and bottom planks are therefore parallel to each other . . .

These planks are bound together by hardwood wooden screws, iron bolts, and iron spikes. There were 67 wooden screws a little under 1½ inches in thickness. The thread on two of the screws, the only ones available for examination, did not seem as if formed with a screw-plate or mechanical contrivance . . . There were angular projections on the timber as if cut with a knife but not sufficiently rough to impede screwing home . . . There were 16 iron bolts. I could not ascertain if the ends had been in the screw-plate . . . They were of the same thickness as the wooden screws . . . There were also a few spikes like the 6 inch spikes we are accustomed to. They were driven at irregular distances and might have been used for subsequent repairs . . . There were therefore 83 screws and bolts holding together an area of about 60 square feet of deck, or whatever part it might have been, constructed (and designed) in the strangest manner . . . It is said that copper bolts were also found, and iron and copper bolts joined together, but I did not see them . . . ('An examination of the mystery wreck of Ruapuke Beach, October 1982.' Auckland Institute and Museum Report.)

Two years before this report was filed a number of the wooden screws referred to were removed by souvenir hunters, as were several of the brass bolts which didn't seem to be in evidence in this 1892 examination. In 1875, of course, Mr Hill had removed a piece of timber which he later found to be teak, and which he subsequently had 'turned in the shape of a ruler, as a souvenir of a pleasant picnic'. Overall, however, there is no way of tracking down what may have originated from the wreck site and what didn't. Any evidence in this regard is largely anecdotal, and impossible to verify.

There were stories about locals using pieces of the wreck timber for various purposes such as farm buildings and the like, and to this end, during

A sketch of unidentified wreckage at Ruapuke Beach showing the multi-layered construction of the hull. It was drawn by Dr R.A. Falla who was born in 1901, and since the wreck was accessible to him only in 1914 and 1919 it was more likely he visited the site as a student in 1919.

(COLLECTION OF THE MUSEUM OF NEW ZEALAND TE PAPA TONGAREWA, NEG. NO. B 010875)

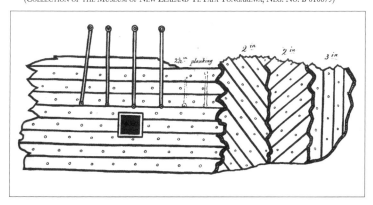

the exposure of 1913–1914, explosives were used in an attempt to loosen the planking for removal. There was a 'willow pattern' plate in the area, said to have originally come from the wreck, but precious little else apparently, for which the same sort of thing could be claimed. Quite simply there do not appear to have ever been any loose objects inside the wreck for anyone to take away in the first place, and there may never have been a complete ship at Ruapuke anyway. This would completely sink the idea that there is still treasure trove to be had from the site.

As for all the coins, medals, buttons, bullets and other sundry small items dug from the sand in the vicinity, and held up by their finders as genuine relics, these can all be dismissed as irrelevant. By sheer coincidence, a number of fully clothed bodies were buried in the surrounding sand dunes about nine decades ago following a severe and fatal epidemic among Maori, and the 'finds' are nothing more than personal effects from several coffins which weathered open and scattered their contents.

Ruapuke Beach: A 'Glory Hole' of Flotsam?

After Mr Hunt had invested a tremendous amount of time and effort in gathering evidence from the Ruapuke wreck site, in interviewing local people capable of helping him with his enquiries, in pursuing numerous clues which seemed to abound in the Raglan/Ruapuke district, and in trying to get to the bottom of a multitude of theories on the subject, it dawned on him, because of the many conflicting accounts he had heard, that there may be more than one wreck out on the lonely beach. An examination of some of the items shown to him as relics 'soon revealed that some of them could not be as old as the wreck in question and must have been flotsam from other wrecks in the vicinity'. When all the evidence is studied, certain anomalies do become apparent. Historian Schnackenberg spoke of *three* layers of laminated timber the hull of the wreck was supposed to consist of. The official from the Auckland Museum in 1892 mentioned *five* layers. A local landowner mentioned *several*. Of all the surviving planking and other pieces of wood said to have come from the wreck, some was later identified as 'an inferior type of pine', some 'teak', and some 'kauri'. The wreck was sometimes described as 'large and massive', right down to small enough for the local Thomson brothers to be able to play on it as it floated free of the beach on the high tide some time during the 1913–1914 showing. An adjacent landowner is positive that the sand in the vicinity of the wreck is less than 2 metres thick and is solid limestone rock beneath that. His contention is that the 'wreck' can have no depth, and may only be a portion of decking.

Mr Hunt compiled a list of 65 ships known to have foundered or to have been wrecked between Waikato Heads and Cape Egmont which 'could, and probably did, contribute wreckage to Ruapuke Beach'. On top of this information should be added further intelligence of wide-ranging implication. A factor glossed over in the past is the effect on our subject beach of Southern Hemisphere ocean currents, and the possibility that, because of them, flotsam may have come from much further afield than just the areas a few dozen kilometres north and south of Ruapuke.

In the years since reliable electronic detectors have been available to treasure hunters, particularly in Britain, much has been learned by these people about coastal sea currents and the effect they have on solid objects discarded or lost in the water. At popular beaches where rings, watches, coins, bracelets and the like are lost by the public and become subject to the influence of the sea, the configuration of tide, moon and wind on any average day drives the water into particular local current patterns, during which solid objects present are picked up in the process and eventually dropped in designated areas known as 'glory holes'. The sand can be clear for hundreds of metres in every direction, but in one small spot – perhaps less than half a metre across – will be found an accumulation of heavy gold and silver objects.

On a grander scale, the same sort of thing happens from ocean to ocean. It is very likely that Ruapuke Beach and surrounding area is the 'glory hole' of the North Island's west coast, and indeed, for a large part of the Southern Hemisphere. One has only to look at the record. In 1906 a sealed bottle thrown overboard by the first officer of the SS *Moravian* near Cape Leeuwin (West Australia) was picked up on Ruapuke Beach. It had travelled 4828 km in 14 months. Numerous other bottles containing messages and 'sent by Aussies' have been found in the general vicinity as well.

In the late 1940s a large anti-shipping mine was washed up. The occurrence was reported to the New Zealand naval authorities who sent a demolition squad to deal with it. Petty Officer Graham-Cameron said after it had been safely detonated that it had come from a minefield laid by a German raider in Bass Strait during the early part of the war. Naval authorities were aware, he said, that the cables anchoring the mines were now corroding through and, though most of them would sink, a few were expected to find their way to Ruapuke. It had proved an uncannily correct prediction. Five or six more did show up in various places between Raglan Heads and the mouth of the Mokau River soon after.

So from Western Australia to Ruapuke Beach for a bottle, and from Bass Strait to the same place for half a dozen Second World War German mines. Has there been any other flotsam of relevance? The historian E.H. Schnackenberg at one time considered the Ruapuke wreck to be nothing much more than a portion of the *Schomberg*, a vessel which came to grief at Cape Otway, Australia, in 1855. In 1866 a piece of this ship was found by miners washed up on the West Coast of the South Island and it was felt that perhaps the wreck at Ruapuke Beach was yet another fragment of this same vessel. So it could yet prove to be if and when it becomes exposed again. Meanwhile we will just have to keep on wondering why people have been describing different methods of construction for what is ostensibly the same piece of wreckage. And why pieces of wood from this supposed one piece of wreckage have been identified at various times as either teak, pine or kauri. We may be dealing with portions of several different ships at our beach – several little testimonies of maritime disasters which occurred not only to the immediate west of New Zealand, but also around the Australian coasts as well – and possibly further afield. Having said this, though, the possibility remains that one or more of the wreck fragments could well be the evidence of primary pre-1769 contact. We can't be sure until further investigation becomes feasible.

In the 1980s the South African Government is said to have conducted experiments with ocean currents by placing floating metallic strips in the sea and tracking them by satellite. And where did most of them end up? You've guessed it. However, approaches for details to South Africa's Council for Scientific and Industrial Research, who in conjunction with the Marine Development Branch of their Department of Environment Affairs conducts such experiments, have met with silence.

The implications become far-reaching even without any details, though. If the bronze name plate prised from the deck of the Ruapuke wreck in 1875 by T.B. Hill is ever found, if its Tamil-like script is placed alongside that on Colenso's bell and found to match it perfectly, if both relics can be shown beyond all doubt to have originated from the same piece of wrecked ship still lying beneath the sands of Ruapuke Beach, it still won't mean very much. It will still not be necessarily proven even then that the wreck and its now-validated relics had a primary association with New Zealand. In the light of some of the things we have just been looking at – the ocean currents (particularly what is known as the 'Tasman Drift'), a variety of material which has floated from as far away as Western Australia to Ruapuke Beach, and specifically the South African experiments – would it not be reasonable for us to assume that the piece of old ship we have been studying may well be of Tamil origin alright, except that its crew likely came to grief on the Australian coast, or even a lonely coast somewhere on a southern portion of the African continent, and nowhere near ours? In which case all material connected with it, and now newly suspected of having only a secondary association with this country, can at last be classified as just that, freeing us up to investigate material and incidents much more likely to help in our quest for non-Polynesians who may have been in New Zealand before 1769.

8

The Spanish and Portuguese in Pre-1769 New Zealand

Interest in a Spanish Presence

Did stray Spanish seafarers come to New Zealand in the 16th century and leave behind wrecked ships in Northland, red hair and blue eyes among Maori, and the inspiration for several Maori folktales? There is no known documentation to support any of these notions. For the last century and a half most of them seem to have survived on a mixture of speculation and sheer wishful thinking and it's simple enough to trace quickly how it all came about.

In 1843 Ernst Dieffenbach suggested that dogs in New Zealand were 'probably first brought here by the Spaniards'. In 1859 A.S. Thomson echoed this, but added that they also brought the first pigs as well. Spain had just recently claimed that the honour of discovering New Zealand should really go to Juan Fernandez who in 1576 was alleged to have sailed from South America to this country in 30 days. Thomson indirectly supported this by saying that, after Magellan's discovery of a western passage to India, Spanish ships touched at New Zealand during their many voyages between Manila and the western seaboard of South America. However, he had more to say on the subject. He went on to draw comparisons between some localised Maori words and their supposed Spanish equivalents, claiming that such linguistic artefacts were a remnant of centuries-old Spanish-Maori interaction. He suggested puke and buque (a ship), pero and perro (a dog), mate and morte (death), and so on. These seductive semantics soon had many people convinced, and for the next 70 years it was fashionable to probe both languages in the search for yet more comparisons. Even as late as 1926 it was still going on. In the *Dominion* of 9 February of that year there was a paragraph which commented on Elsdon Best's interest in the subject. The essential question posed was: 'Are these words merely coincidences, or is it possible that the first ship the Maoris saw was a Spanish buque?'

Throughout the 1880s writers and scholars posed the questions: 'why stop with the Spanish? Why couldn't *anyone* have been here before Cook?' This kind of thinking reached a climax on 31 July 1889, when at a meeting of the Wellington Philosophical Society people like Smith, Tregear, Maskell, Kirk and others recorded the following comments: 'there was room for any number of ships to have touched at New Zealand' (prior to 1769) – 'the captains of these ships were not allowed, except in special cases like Tasman's, to publish records of their voyages' – and – 'in the archives of Lisbon and Amsterdam there might be found numbers of such unpublished ship's logs' – and so on. A motion was passed that a letter-writing campaign to the institutions be undertaken in an effort to track down these logs. But none ever materialised.

As the 20th century dawned, interest in an early Spanish presence in New Zealand quickly faded as first the Boer War and then the Great War of 1914–1918 rose to become top priorities for the nation. When all the fighting was over things weren't the same any more. During the 1920s and 1930s a new type of scholar was emerging – one who had a strong aversion to unbridled speculation when it came to historical matters, and one who wasn't going to accept anything at all unless there was full and complete documentation to back it up. This, of course, meant that speculation about the Spanish soon became unfashionable. So much so that when a student approached the National Library in 1967 seeking details of a Spanish presence in New Zealand he was told: 'I have found very few references to the theory that there was European contact with New Zealand before Tasman . . . Modern authorities do not take the theory seriously, and recent publications make no reference to it at all.'

But nothing stays the same.

The attitudinal tide began turning the other way again in 1982 following the first of a series of discoveries in the Dargaville area (outlined in Chapter 1). First, Mr Hilliam spotted what appeared to be the wreck of a caravel in the breakers off Bayly's Beach while flying over in an aircraft. 'It was broad in the stern and then narrowed to a rounded bow,' Hilliam said. 'The stub of the mainmast could be seen, as could the break in the sheerline where the poop-deck met the gunwhale.' Second, planking attached to a curved bow frame by the square peg trundling method – unique to old Spanish ships – was found in a mussel bed in the Kaipara Harbour. The timber was identified as *Lagerstromeia*, which occurs only in a belt between southern India and the Philippines where the Spanish were once based. Third, the shape of a large ship has been detected by electronic means in otherwise clear silt 12 metres below where stock now feed on lush grass.

The finds have not only attracted official Spanish interest, but are probably one of the principal causes of many in the academic community now saying: 'We don't altogether discount a pre-Tasman Spanish presence in New Zealand but would need to see good solid documentary evidence before we are convinced.'

Time now to take a look at some of the material which has encouraged the idea of a Spanish presence in New Zealand prior to Tasman. There are several factors involved – apart from recent discoveries in Northland.

The *San Lesmes*

No other missing ship in Pacific maritime history has spawned as much speculation as the *San Lesmes*. In company with three other vessels it left Spain in July 1525, bound for the Pacific via Cape Horn. But barely had the small fleet emerged from the Straits of Magellan than a violent north-easterly storm scattered the four craft, and, when calm returned, the *San Lesmes* was missing. So did it sink? Or did it continue on alone westward into the great unknown ocean? For four and a half centuries its eventual fate has been the cause of endless speculation and debate.

There are two broad schools of thought on the matter. Led by Roger Hervé, there are those who maintain the *San Lesmes* came straight on over to New Zealand. Objectors to this idea point to prevailing wind conditions met by any ship emerging from the Straits of Magellan as working against the notion. They question why any captain would want to struggle against strong westerly winds in the latitude of Cape Horn when all he had to do was sail up the coast of Chile for a few days and dodge them. But Hervé insists that

A surprisingly small vessel, the caravel was favoured by the Spanish in the 16th century for exploration and discovery work. Although a good sailer, at least one is thought to have come to grief on a New Zealand shore.

(COURTESY OF THE SPANISH NAVAL MUSEUM, MADRID)

between June and September each year gale-force winds from either the east or south-east often blow south of the Cape and that, having been driven down there by the storm, the *San Lesmes* was in a perfect position to run before them all the way to New Zealand.

However, Langdon and others choose a different scenario (see Langdon's *The Lost Caravel Re-explored*, 1988). After the discovery of several cannon on a reef in the Tuamotu Archipelago, Langdon asserted that these weapons constituted the first in a series of clues left by the caravel as it fumbled its way around the Pacific. From Tuamotu it proceeded to Anaa, thence past Tahiti and on to Ra'iatea. After repairing their ship the men decided to head back to Spain via the Cape of Good Hope but 'lying athwart the Cape's latitude,' Langdon says, 'on a south-western course . . . there was one substantial and unknown obstacle – the North Island of New Zealand.' Langdon believes that when the vessel struck New Zealand unexpectedly the crew stayed here and settled down with Polynesian wives.

Juan Fernandez

Once claimed by the Spanish to have discovered New Zealand in 1576, Fernandez presents us with a real enigma. The biggest problem with his story is that he was alleged to have sailed from Chile to New Zealand in just 30 days, a feat which would have been near-miraculous for a sailing ship in the 16th century. Many have seen the voyage as improbable because of the 11,265-kilometre distance separating the two countries, but the point should be made that Fernandez was no ordinary sailor. He already had a reputation for cunning navigation and speed on the water which he earned on the well-known Lima to Chile run where weather and current allowed a good speed one way but on the return Chile to Lima haul things were much more difficult. Fernandez discovered that by sailing a certain distance out from the coast on this particular leg a surprising amount of time could be saved. He was so fast on these journeys in fact that he soon came to the attention of the Inquisition who suspected him of employing some kind of occult assistance. He survived the enquiry that followed but at the time couldn't help picking up a nickname that was to dog him for the rest of his life: 'Witch of the Pacific'.

Some scholars who have been looking through the Juan Fernandez material have suggested that he went nowhere – that he simply sailed away from Chile for a month and came back to the American continent telling people he had been to someplace which perhaps he hadn't. This would be a simple way to deal with the problem posed by the man and his claims, but is hardly very objective.

Why would Fernandez do such a thing? As the tool of a patron who had a grand design to set up either a commercial venture, or else a settlement in some new land, he would have been totally accountable to him for every moment spent at sea. He spoke of discovering a large green land to the west of Chile filled with noble and hospitable people, and featuring many rivers. New Zealand appears to be the only land mass which qualifies in all these respects. The Spanish navigator kept the latitude and longitude of his discovery a secret, and while having every intention of returning to 'New Zealand' died in Chile before the opportunity arose.

Red Hair and Blue Eyes

An integral part of New Zealand folklore is that Spaniards were originally responsible for the reddish hair and blue eyes sometimes seen among Maori. Perhaps they were, and perhaps they weren't, but Ernst Dieffenbach showed how easily these traits could come about. When he visited a Marlborough whaling station in the early 1840s he supplied us with the best contemporary description we have of the appearance of the offspring of unions between European men and full-blooded Maori women.

> The whalers received us with a hearty welcome wherever we came. They are about forty in number, and all live with native women. Their offspring, of whom I counted twenty-one in Te-awa-iti, have finely cast countenances, and their features remind us little of the admixture of a coloured race; the skin is not so dark as that of the inhabitants of the south of France; they generally inherit from their mother the large and fine eye and the dark glossy hair; there are, however, *many individuals with flaxen hair and blue eyes*. (*Travels in New Zealand*, 1843. Emphasis added.)

From the above it could probably be inferred that the red-haired, blue-eyed Maori noticed in New Zealand by the very first commentators to write about the subject – at a time when there had barely been a chance for interracial contact – must have acquired these colourings only per medium of a much earlier European input.

Dr A.S. Thomson wrote in 1859, speaking of the Maori race as a whole:

... some have hair with a rusty red tinge. This red tinge which is likewise found in the head-hair of other Polynesian races, has been ascribed to the use of alkaline washes, but *such is not the case among the New Zealanders*. [Emphasis added.]

Some recent scholars have been prepared to admit the theoretical possibility of an outside, pre-1769 influence on Maori. In his book *A History of New Zealand* (1988), Keith Sinclair wrote:

'Classical' Maori culture, . . . though still Polynesian, was strikingly different from that of the early inhabitants . . . There was now a formidable array of weapons, . . . The landscape was dominated, especially in the north, by the pallisaded, terraced hilltop fortresses, the pa.

The reasons for these changes, which could have been the result either of local cultural evolution or *of alien intrusion* . . . are unknown. [Emphasis added.]

The Dieppe Maps

In 1983, a small book with a very big title – *Chance Discovery of Australia and New Zealand by Portuguese and Spanish Navigators between 1521 and 1528* – proclaimed in essence that 'the credit for the discovery of Australia and New Zealand by Europeans rightly belongs, not to Dutch, but to Spanish and Portuguese navigators.' The work was a translation from the French by New Zealand's Professor John Dunmore, who felt that 'English-speaking scholars

---

OPPOSITE: One of the 'Dieppe' maps, handpainted on vellum by the Frenchman Pierre Hamon in 1568, 74 years before Tasman 'discovered' New Zealand. The land mass in the bottom right-hand corner is 'Jave-la-Grande', believed to be the countries of New Guinea, Australia and New Zealand lumped together. The sharp-pointed piece of land intruding into the border of the map is 'Cap Frimose' – the 'beautiful Cape' – the East Cape of the North Island, and just south of this are the indents of Hawke's Bay and Cook Strait. The map is 'upside down': when navigators in the 16th century sailed south they invariably spoke of 'going up' into 'higher' latitudes. (COURTESY OF THE NATIONAL MARITIME MUSEUM, LONDON)

and others interested in early discoveries' would benefit by having access to the ideas of the French author concerned. This was Roger Hervé, for many years map keeper at the Bibliotheque Nationale de Paris, where after 'close and tireless analysis of every chart still extant', he was led to 'formulate a series of hypotheses about early knowledge of the whole South-west Pacific' – including New Zealand.

Working with about 200 holograph 'maps' representing the first ever attempts at French sea charts, Hervé chanced upon information which 'relates to Portuguese and Spanish navigations in Australian and New Zealand waters between 1521 and 1528', and 'which have remained secret or unsuspected until recently.' But the task has not been made any easier by the material Hervé has had to work with. Part factual, part fantasy, he states that the 'documentation . . . is essentially amateurish, the work of semi literate pilots, drawn up for sailors who were themselves virtually illiterate.'

Despite all the seeming drawbacks, however, some fairly radical information appears to have been uncovered. We can only briefly summarise this here, but the main points are:

- In 1542 a map produced by one John Rotz was so above average Hervé speculated that the map-maker seemed to have had at his disposal 'precise hydrographic information about shores that were still unknown – namely . . . the entire New Zealand archipelago . . .'

- The map-maker and his associates may also have had 'precise geographical co-ordinates (latitude and longitude) for the following points, implying a prolonged stay in those areas: the East Cape of New Zealand in the North Island . . .' (for one). This is the 'Fremose' or 'Frimosa' of the old map-makers, that is to say 'the fine Cape which is in the austral land . . .'.

- On some Dieppe-style charts the New Zealand archipelago appears as one great island called 'La Joncade', and is situated in an approximately correct latitudinal position. It will be recalled that in 1642 Tasman with his chart was half way towards treating New Zealand as one land mass also. And in 1550 the Portuguese seemed to have had trouble recognising Cook Strait for what it was. They simply marked the area in the charts as the 'Gulf of the Portuguese', suggesting that they too probably saw Aotearoa as one continuous piece of land.

- In his *Voyages Avantureux* (1559), Jean Alfonse, one of explorer Jacques Cartier's men, wrote the following cryptic words: 'Now we come out of the Strait of Magaillant . . . and met a coast that trends north and south . . . In this eastern land are seen many pines and good rivers. The people one saw here were white and of good height'. Hervé believes this land was New Zealand, and that later references to a mystical 'Island of White Men' were allusions to it also.

- Hervé postulates a different fate for the *San Lesmes* than Langdon does. Supporting his ideas by continual reference to the maps, and by an astute process of evaluation and interpretation, he has the lost caravel being blown down towards the Antarctic ice after its separation from the fleet, and then clawing its way slowly northwards again via New Zealand's subantarctic islands. After striking the coast of New Zealand somewhere to the south of East Cape Hervé asserts that the Spaniards stayed long enough 'to carry out some fairly precise astronomical observations' – particularly as to the exact location of East Cape – and that all this data later appeared on John Rotz's 1542 map.

  In summing up his argument for this particular scenario, Hervé said:

> Thus also can be solved the mystery of the Spanish helmet discovered in 1906 in Wellington Harbour, and of the widespread traditions found among Maoris of the arrival of strangers long before Tasman, Cook or Marion du Fresne. The striking Maori likenesses in some illustrations of the Le Testu atlas cease to be puzzling, and Alfonse's repeated utterances about one or more great islands in the Pacific – 'one has a coastline of more than 60 leagues, good harbours . . . well-populated with white people of good height' – are explained, not as the author suggests by Magellan's well-known voyage, but in the unintended drifting and sailing of the *San Lesmes* to New Zealand . . .

Hervé had reason to believe that after her sojourn in New Zealand, the San Lesmes proceeded over to Australia where the famous so-called 'Mohogany Ship' stranded among the Warnambool dunes on the coast of Victoria marks the end of its journey. The crew then struck north on foot, and after an unspecified period of perils and adventures finally reached civilisation.

The 'Spanish' Helmet

Some time in 1906, although the exact date and circumstances are themselves a bit of a mystery, the Wellington Harbour dredge brought up an ancient steel helmet and round cannon shot from the sea bed while working off the wharves. For many years the objects lay in the Dominion Museum unidentified until finally in 1963 photographs of the helmet were sent to England for authoritative study. There it was determined that it was of a type known as a 'morion', and was of Spanish origin. Its date of use was tentatively set at AD 1560 to 1580 – give or take a few decades.

So how did it come to be in Wellington Harbour? Was it brought here by 19th-century British immigrants as a souvenir and accidentally or otherwise dropped overboard from a ship, as suggested in an article in the *Evening Post* of 27 June 1953? The same article pointed out that, up to that year, no published Spanish records appeared to exist which made any specific mention of a visit by a Spanish ship to a country with the characteristics of New Zealand. It conceded, though, that there may be some documents still to be unearthed in a Spanish monastery which could yet indicate such a possibility.

Or did the helmet come from a Spanish ship commanded by Juan Fernandez in 1576, as hypothesised by the author of an article in the *Dominion* of 28 February 1924? Judging by the corroded state of the helmet it would appear at first glance to have been in the sea far longer than a few short decades immediately prior to 1906. The article said there was no known extant report by Fernandez on such a journey to New Zealand and the only known source for such an idea is a memorial to the King of Spain which Don Luis Arias drew up at the insistence of the Franciscan mission on the west coast of South America. Arias mentioned a Pacific voyage from the coast of

Chile, and spoke of light-coloured, or 'white people' encountered by Fernandez. The article concluded with a discussion of the significance of Spanish jealousy of the intrusion of other nations into the Pacific.

Other writers have offered explanations for the helmet's presence in Wellington Harbour also. Robert Langdon (1988) says that it 'could have come from the *San Lesmes*', in 1526. France's Roger Hervé agrees. He says that by placing the *San Lesmes* in New Zealand waters in the 1520s the mystery of the Spanish helmet 'can be solved'.

Another writer goes further. In his book *Trail Blazers of New Zealand* (1974), Nadoo Balantyne-Scott, after accepting the idea that a 16th-century Spanish ship may have entered Wellington Harbour, says '. . . it is also reasonable to assume that the Spaniards came ashore for at least a bit of a walkabout before sailing on . . .' and 'that would place the date of the first European to set foot on New Zealand soil about 200 years ahead of Captain Cook.'

However, modern authorities are not happy with any of these ideas. Recent research (see Robin Watt's article in *National Museum Records*) is cited as 'proof' that the helmet couldn't have lain on the sea floor all that time and that it was much more likely to have been lost overboard from a vessel in more recent times.

East Coast Spaniards

Finally, a cautionary note for those who see the East Coast of the North Island as being the best place to hunt for clues of a pre-1769 Spanish presence in New Zealand. After all, this is where most of the folklore on the subject is centred. And it is also the area suspected of featuring in the Dieppe maps, and one or two 16th-century 'sea ruttiers' as well. Pre-Cook traditions about contact with white people in ships exist here, and there is also a disproportionate concentration of red/fair-haired, green/blue-eyed individuals among Coast Maori. But all is not as it seems.

As well as these things there are many other clues of an early Spanish presence. In fact, *too many* clues. Almost any East Coast Maori family – particularly those living in the Waiapu and Tikitiki areas – will acknowledge some sort of Spanish blood in their veins. Many of them even have Spanish names, or else their forebears have had them. From Antonio to Miguel, and Alfonso to Juanita, it is possible to identify up to 30 different Spanish forenames among the people there. There are also Spanish and Portuguese surnames going back six or eight generations or more. Maori speak of each other as having a 'Spanish' temper, or else a 'Manuel' head, or a 'Manuel' forehead. It has also been known for respected old ladies to be addressed as 'Senorita'; one, in fact, had the title 'Queen of the Spaniards' bestowed upon her some generations back. So what is the explanation for all this?

We must turn to Robert McConnell's book *Olive Branches* (1980) to find out. Here we see that 95 per cent of the above can be attributed to a lone Spaniard who settled on the coast in the 1830s. His name was Manuel José, a Castillian, who had spent time at sea until coming ashore to set up as a trader. He eventually had five wives from among Ngati Porou women, and his descendants today exceed 6300. But just why a Spaniard should arrive on the East Coast out of the blue years before other Europeans came to settle is a bit of a mystery. McConnell says:

> We do not know whether he was following some vision, whether a spirit of adventure led him, or even if he was perhaps fleeing a haunting past, but whatever the motive, he started a new life for himself, when he arrived in the Waiapu.

There is other speculation too. It is thought that he may have had access to family documents describing Spanish visits to the East Coast 300 years before his arrival there, and that these had fired his imagination to the extent that he determined to come among these people to see for himself. Whether log books or later memoirs, they must have been detailed enough to paint a favourable picture of East Coast Maori and their environment, to have motivated him to the degree necessary.

The extended Manuel José family in New Zealand also has early Portuguese and Brazilian connections and these have never been seriously investigated; indeed, back 'home' somewhere could be the documentation recently sought after by our own Dr Phyllis Herda. As a relevant footnote to this, it is interesting to observe that some East Coast Maori bear the forename 'Fernandez'.

Manual José at Waiapu in the 1830s had long reddish hair and green eyes – traits he has passed on to many of his descendants. They are also traits which were present on the Coast centuries before he arrived. If one Spaniard can be responsible for 6300 descendants in one and a half centuries, how many would several shiploads of them have left after four and a half centuries? It is entirely possible that almost every Maori on the whole of the East Coast has a few corpuscles in their veins which can be credited to some early Spanish seaman or other.

Generally speaking, though, the academic community today tends to reject the idea of a pre-Cook Spanish presence in New Zealand because of a lack of hard evidence. However, at least one of their number has been tantalised enough by the possibility to do something tangible. Dr Phyllis Herda, a history lecturer at Victoria University, recently spent time combing libraries in Britain, Spain and the Americas, in the hope of finding a first-hand account which would confirm the 1576 visit to New Zealand of Juan Fernandez. She was unsuccessful, but not discouraged enough to give up. She believes that if the documentary evidence does exist it is likely to be held in a private collection somewhere, where access could be difficult.

With regard to Dr Herda's quest, media accounts speak of the trail as 'fizzling out', or else 'going cold', and Dr Herda herself says that at this point she really needs good first-hand information if any future progress is to be made. Meanwhile, although the whole exercise boils down to a matter of possibilities, rather than probabilities, she is still interested enough to keep on looking. And no one could ask for more than that.

9

The Dutch Connection

Weighing Tasman's History

The folklore which has attached itself to the Dutch discovery of New Zealand paints a somewhat different picture from that contained in the written record. The material suggests that either Tasman *did* come ashore in New Zealand in 1642 contrary to whatever he wrote in his ship's log, or that other Dutchmen did the same thing a year or two later. Whatever the case, there is good reason to believe that land battles did occur between Maori and European seafarers during the 17th century in the Nelson-Marlborough area.

We find the first hint that all is not well with the official version of events in the writings of historian Dr A.S. Thomson who in 1859 said:

> He . . . who weighs Tasman's history for the sake of truth, must not forget that only one side of the narrative has come down to us. (*The Story of New Zealand*)

What did Thomson mean by this? What was the other side of the narrative he seemed to be hinting at? The side that was missing, and which was necessary to get at the truth. Was he expressing misgivings about the version of Tasman's visit to New Zealand as recorded in the Dutch log? It would seem so. And before we have finished finding out why we will likely be sharing these same misgivings ourselves.

The other side of the narrative referred to by Thomson is a dossier of information which can be grouped under three headings – South Island Maori tradition, the scurvy factor, and a critical assessment of Tasman and his writings. The sum total of all this is a direct challenge to what is contained in the log of the *Heemskerck*.

No likeness of Tasman's two ships are known to have survived apart from that depicted in the rough sketch shown here. The *Heemskerck* (foreground) was a 'war yacht' of 120 tons displacement while the *Zeehan* was a 'fluyt' of 200 tons. (COLLECTION OF THE MUSEUM OF NEW ZEALAND TE PAPA TONGAREWA, NEG. NO. B 012377)

Maori Tradition

In his book *Kei Puta Te Wairau* (1957), W.J. Elvy has recorded an ancient piece of pre-Cook folklore which is quite fascinating. It concerns the sudden arrival of a ship at the top of the South Island manned by sailors 'of fair complexion' (Europeans), with a few present who were 'darker than the Maori' (Negro). Many ships involved in early exploration work in the Pacific usually always had one or two Negro aboard – they were even present on some of Cook's ships – and it's interesting to see the fact preserved like this in a centuries-old tradition.

A landing party came ashore from the ship looking for fresh food and water and for a time all went well. But after enjoying the hospitality of Maori a quarrel erupted when the sailors tried to take some of the local women back to the ship. Maori objected strongly, and fighting broke out. Men were killed on both sides, the sailors beat a hasty retreat, and the ship sailed away into apparent oblivion.

The most interesting feature of the account, however, is the Maori description of the battle itself. We are told that the newcomers were wearing 'shiny coats that could turn off the Maori stone weapons', and that they were well armed with 'spears', and 'battle axes'. You don't have to be very bright to work out that the European intruders were wearing battle armour, and that they were armed with pikes, cutlasses, and possibly firearms.

When James Cook asked Maori at Queen Charlotte Sound in 1770, 'have you ever seen or heard of a ship such as ours on this coast before?' one particular answer he received is relevant to this chapter. Cook's Maori informant told him that according to his ancestors two ships 'much larger than theirs' had once come to that particular part of the world and that four of the strangers were killed *'upon their landing'*. The likely date of the event in the middle of the 17th century caused Professor Beaglehole to observe of this story that it 'may just possibly be a very garbled version' of Tasman's visit in 1642.

A third piece of Maori tradition relating to Tasman's visit has been confirmed by the discovery of 17th-century relics to back it up. Details were released at a meeting of the Nelson Historical Society on 26 November 1963.

The story concerns a retired engine driver by the name of Frank Robertson who, together with his two sons, moved to Wainui in the Nelson province and leased from Maori most of the flat land there. At Wainui, Robertson senior became very friendly with a Maori known as Paramena with whom he shared many a problem, and spent endless hours discussing old times. The friendship blossomed to the extent that secrets were shared, and when one day a message reached Robertson that Paramena was dying and wanted to see him quickly Robertson hastened to the bedside of his old friend.

Paramena disclosed that he was the last surviving member of the Tumata-kokiri tribe (with whom Tasman came into contact) and that there was ancient information he wished to pass on before he died. He explained that when members of his tribe attacked the white crew of a visiting European ship – which he supposed was that of the Tasman expedition – Maori prevailed to the extent that they were able to capture a quantity of arms which had been in the possession of the slain sailors.

The victorious war party took the arms back to Wainui Pa where a dispute arose among the chiefs as to who should own them. The matter was referred to the tohunga who, Solomon-like, decreed that nobody should. He placed a tapu on them and ordered that they be buried instead. Paramena knew where the burial had taken place and he explained to Robertson in great detail the exact location of the spot.

When Robertson arrived back home and discussed the matter with his family they all concluded that Paramena must have been delirious and had talked nonsense. And so the matter may have rested indefinitely. But some years later the paddock mentioned as the burial place was stumped and ploughed and to everyone's surprise two musket barrels were ploughed up by Frank's son, Morris, at the spot indicated. Robertson junior then remembered that Paremena had made specific reference to a 'cutlass', and on digging around the area he found that also. The bronze handle and guard was in excellent repair but the steel blade was badly corroded and in trying to extract it from the ground the ancient relic broke in two.

So what do you do with two musket barrels and a cutlass you know are quite likely associated with Abel Tasman? Today you would rush them straight to a museum as fast as your little feet could carry you but in 1910 when the event occurred the items were little more than curios. Morris put the relics in the corner of his cow shed but shortly afterwards they disappeared.

He suspected that a college drawing master named Huddlestone – who was camping nearby – had 'souvenired' them for the school museum which was being formed about that time. And so it proved to be. Enquiries revealed the following entry in the museum register: '1910. Presented by Mr F.C. Huddleston. Two musket barrels and a sword, said to have been dug up near Takaka.' A later search failed to find the items in the museum and a possible reason is that at one stage the museum room was required for a classroom and the exhibits stored in cases and transferred to back sheds where they were unprotected, and many were lost.

There are other traditions from the Nelson-Marlborough area but although they are rather sparse in detail they do at least firm up the idea of Europeans in the Cook Strait region before Cook's arrival.

The Scurvy Factor

The main feature of all the traditions is that the fair-skinned visitors invariably came ashore, and there was always fighting and death. And this leads us on to the next consideration. *Why* did they always come ashore? It was well known in maritime circles that 'the southern regions are peopled by fierce savages', as Tasman's superiors wrote in 1642. So why willingly put yourself at risk by going among them? The answer is – there was simply no choice. By the time any ship arrived here up to about Cook's time a good proportion of the crew was either dead from scurvy, or else extremely ill from it. And an old nautical saying had it that 'it was better to run the risk of being clubbed to death and eaten by the New Zealanders than to have all your teeth fall out through scurvy'. So that is why mariners were always keen to get ashore quickly; the pressing need for fresh greens and water overrode everything else.

It we take a close look at two early documented voyages to this country – de Surville in 1769, and du Fresne in 1772 – and study the effect scurvy had on each of these particular expeditions, we will then become better equipped to catch Tasman out again.

When de Surville arrived here in 1769, 60 of his crew were already dead from scurvy with the remainder being very close to death. The navigator was only 53 days out from his home port of Pondicherry when the first men began dying. Prior to touching at New Zealand he had been at sea 58 days since leaving the Solomon Islands and his last source of fresh food and water, and men were dying daily again when the New Zealand coast was sighted. It was an all-round disaster. De Surville hadn't originally intended calling in to New Zealand but reaching here soon became a matter of sheer survival. There weren't enough fit men aboard to carry out the most basic tasks and things were so bad that one of the ship's officers (Monneron) wrote:

... a few more days without landing and the vessel 'St. Jean Baptiste' would never have left New Zealand coasts except by a miracle.

Getting ashore for fresh food and water was the *only* priority the survivors had.

A more relevant comparison would be the Marion du Fresne expedition which in 1772 came in to New Zealand on exactly the same track Tasman took. Du Fresne left Capetown on 3 December 1771, and after 68 days tried unsuccessfully to get fresh food and water at Tasmania. By the time he reached New Zealand, scurvy had so firmly established itself that almost everyone on board was either dying, or else already dead. Du Fresne was also desperate to get ashore. He set up a hospital camp in the Bay of Islands to revive the sick and like de Surville before him could not have sailed any further without stopping.

So what about Tasman? His expedition took place more than 120 years before de Surville and du Fresne. And because he lived in a much more primitive era the incidence of scurvy aboard his ships would have been much more severe, and his hope of combating it without landing much less than the two Frenchmen. Since they suffered so terribly on the very eve of a scurvy breakthrough, how much more must Tasman have suffered?

When the Dutchman arrived in New Zealand in 1642 he had been at sea 66 days – long past the time when scurvy would have been taking its toll, and when men around him would have been dying. The average time at sea for scurvy to cause death was 60 days, sometimes a lot less, and at 66 days Tasman would have been in all sorts of trouble. So when he wrote on 13 December 1642 that 'we resolved to touch at the said land as quickly as at all possible' there was more than a hint of desperation in the statement. The fact was he was facing disaster. The men were in the position of *having to land immediately* for fresh greens and water to save any more from dying. Tasman on that day would have been in exactly the same position as de Surville and du Fresne, both of whom were forced to take everyone ashore to revive them.

Yet what do we find in Tasman's journal? A scenario which stretches belief to the very limits. By the time he left New Zealand on 6 January 1643, still

The alleged likeness of Abel Janszoon Tasman, along with all others noted in numerous books, and on banknotes and postage stamps, are copied from three original portraits held in Australian institutions. But recent research by the Dutch government now indicates that none of them appear to be authentic representations of the man. This is not surprising: if this was an authentic likeness it would be out of place with all other documentation associated with Tasman and his voyage.

allegedly without landing, he had been at sea a staggering 90 days, and more than 100 before finally reaching fresh food and water elsewhere. By then all humans aboard both ships would have long since been dead of scurvy.

Assessments of Tasman and his Writings

So does this mean that Tasman falsified some of the entries in his journal, or was somewhat less than careful about what he wrote in it? We'll let others answer this question.

In June 1643, the Tasman expedition finally arrived back in Batavia after a 10-month voyage. There was no hero's welcome. No fat bonus for each of the crew. The whole enterprise had been a failure. The disappointment of Tasman's masters was neatly expressed in a note sent to Holland later in the year (McNab, Vol. 1, 1914):

> We have, however, observed that the said commander [Tasman] has been somewhat remiss in investigating the situation, confirmation, and nature of the lands discovered, and of the natives inhabiting the same, and, as regards the main point, has left everything to be more closely inquired into by more industrious successors.

More than a century after Tasman's death further derogatory statements were still being made about him:

> What he says about the country does not seem to be very clear, and appears to me to be false on certain points.

You can't get much blunter than that. These words were written in 1769 by a French naval officer (Pottier de L'Horme) with de Surville's expedition to New Zealand when in the vicinity of the Three Kings Islands.

Later, the two ships of du Fresne's 1772 expedition had actually nominated the Three Kings as a rendezvous point in the event they became separated but another French Officer (Roux) wrote that if a separation had occurred 'we should have been greatly misled' (by Tasman's descriptions). In a journal entry for 8 April 1772, Roux also wrote:

> At first we could hardly believe it was the group, because there were only large rocks, whereas Tasman, the Dutch navigator who discovered them in 1643, gave quite another description of them . . . It will be seen that this navigator has made some very erroneous statements . . . (ibid.)

Another journal keeper on the same expedition (de Clesmeur) also recorded his disapproval of Tasman's unconscientious style. He referred to:

> . . . The so-called Kings Islands which we found to be very different from the description given them by Abel Tasman. (ibid.)

The most damning assessment of Tasman has occurred in our time. To mark the 350th anniversary of Tasman's voyage to New Zealand the Dutch government commissioned an in-depth study of the navigator through its Ministry of Foreign Affairs. The result in 1992 was a hard-hitting but objective eye-opener. The *real* Tasman emerged as a 'fearful subaltern', and 'dishonest', and one who 'had tried to falsify the record . . . to avoid problems with his superiors'.

As well as this, it was revealed that all documentation associated with the man and his voyages wasn't all that it seemed either. For example, the muster rolls which would have provided a full list of those taking part in Tasman's expedition 'have not survived', and the logs of his next expedition – around northern Australia in 1644 – are 'missing' too. By failing to discover Torres Strait on that ocassion 'Tasman provided an incorrect answer to the main question the expedition had been sent out to solve'. There are no surviving logs of his two ships *Heemskerck* and *Zeehan* either. These 'disappeared' on his return to Batavia in 1643. Tasman wrote a draft report from 'notes' to replace them, and it too 'disappeared'. What he has attached his signature to in the photograph of the log on the next page is a copy of a copy of the *Heemskerck*'s log and shouldn't necessarily be taken at face value.

For more than two centuries various writers have voiced their disquiet about these things and 'smelt a rat' – especially insofar as Tasman's version of events at Golden Bay is concerned. W. Pember Reeves wrote in 1899:

'Tasman's account – *which I take leave to doubt* [emphasis added] – makes the attack senselessly wanton and unprovoked.' Cook never had this trouble. Not once was he subjected to a 'senselessly wanton and unprovoked attack'. On the contrary, the Maori he met were more interested in trading fish for metal goods and fabrics. The Maori attack on Tasman was more likely in retaliation for something untoward he or his men did ashore.

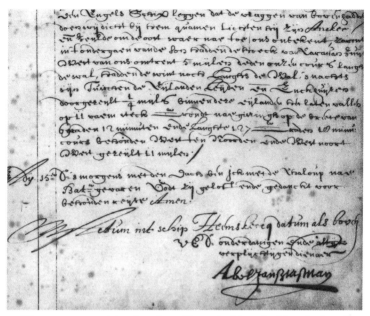

There are no surviving logs from Tasman's ships, the *Heemskerck* and *Zeehan*. This 'log' from the *Heemskerck*, signed by Tasman, is a copy of a copy. (Courtesy of the Algemeen Rijksarchief, The Hague)

A Doctored Log?

So let us now draw all these elements together. They are: the misgivings of Dr Thomson in 1859, a wealth of Maori tradition which speaks of Europeans ashore in the Nelson-Marlborough area before Cook, the discovery of Tasman artefacts buried near Takaka, the scurvy factor, the dissatisfaction of Tasman's Batavian masters, the derogatory comments by French naval officers about parts of Tasman's journal – all speak of only two things. First, a man mis-cast in a role he was unable to handle; Tasman was simply not explorer material. Second, a landing ashore by the Dutch long before Cook arrived.

It was quite common practice in maritime circles to doctor the ship's log. Entries were often made more to please the ship's owner later than to be a record of the truth. When Tasman first set out on his voyage he took with him a very specific and detailed list of instructions designed to cover almost any contingency. The Dutch East India Company was nothing if not thorough. They thought of everything. One instruction read:

> You will prudently prevent all manner of insolence and all arbitrary action on the part of our men against the nations discovered, and take due care that no injury be done them in their houses, gardens, vessels, their property, *their wives* . . . [Emphasis added.]

If Tasman and his men were the star players in Elvy's tradition almost all the above rules were broken. But you can't write things like that in the log. So with the connivance of several of his officers, because it was a consensus-run expedition, it seems a version of events was recorded in the ship's journal which showed the Dutch blameless, and Maori entirely at fault.

And that about sums it up. A suspect journal maintaining no Dutch landing in New Zealand versus a number of factors suggesting the exact opposite. Will it ever be possible to know the truth regarding early Dutch involvement with this country?

10

The Writings of James Cook

Cook's Question to Maori

During the course of his visits to New Zealand between 1769 and 1777 Captain James Cook repeatedly posed a rather curious question to Maori: 'Have you ever seen or heard of a ship such as ours on this coast before?' To us there doesn't seem to be much point to an enquiry of this nature. Cook must have been perfectly aware that the only other European to come to this country before him was Tasman in 1642 . . . mustn't he? So why continually seek details of some other ship? What grounds did he have for wanting to know about earlier unknown navigators who may have preceded him to these shores? *Something* must have prompted the question. And the short answer for now is that something did.

We find the first clue in this regard in the journal of Sir Joseph Banks. Sailing down the east coast of the South Island in February 1770 with Cook, and after contemplating the grandeur of the Southern Alps, he wrote:

> We [that is, he and Cook] once more cherished strong hopes that we had at last completed our wishes and that this was absolutely a part of the Southern Continent especially as *we* [that is, he and Cook] had seen a hint thrown out in some books that the Dutch not contented with Tasman's discoveries had afterwards sent other ships (plural) who took the land [New Zealand] upon the same latitude as he made it in . . . [Emphasis added.]

In other words, Cook and Banks had been discussing Dutch visits to New Zealand which appear to have taken place *after* Tasman's 1642 fiasco. So this would be one possible reason for Cook's question to Maori. But there is more.

After leaving New Zealand in 1770 the Cook expedition sailed across the Tasman to New South Wales and proceeded to probe its way up the east coast. But some of Cook's actions during this part of the journey have led one or two

Australian writers to suggest that far from groping his way northward into the unknown he was using 16th-century Portuguese charts to guide him.

In her book *The Captain Cook Myth Exploded* (1981), Jillian Robertson poses the question: 'Did Captain Cook have a map of the northern coast of Queensland' on his one and only visit to the east coast of Australia in 1770?' She suggests it is likely he was carrying at least one map 'based on secret Portuguese charts smuggled out of Lisbon' in the 16th century. She points out that of the six different Dieppe maps depicting part of the southern hemisphere 'all show an extensive country situated where Australia is'. And because Cook's was essentially a scientific expedition it would have been carried out 'with as much preparation and planning as possible' making it 'unlikely that any available map which might have been useful would have been overlooked'. What's more, it's not as though the English were unaware of the Portuguese-based charts. King Henry VIII of England is said to have had the Rotz version in his possession more than 200 years before Cook set sail.

The factors which encourage the idea of ancient maps in Cook's possession are (a), his bestowal of the name 'Botany Bay' to a spot which was already marked 'Coste des Herbaiges' (Coast of Vegetation) on the charts (b), the use of the term 'Great Barrier Reef' in connection with the treacherous stretch of coral known as 'Coste dangereuse' to the Portuguese and (c), when Cook's ship became holed on this particular reef on 11 June 1770, instead of making for the nearest shore to effect repairs, as most people would have done, or retracing his steps back to a known beach he might have just recently passed, he pressed on instead north-west into the unknown 'towards a coast he could not see, towards land which might not even exist, which might turn out to be worse than anything experienced before', to quote K.G. McIntyre (*The Secret Discovery of Australia*, 1977). In any event, Cook reached the shelter of Cooktown Harbour – a spot, he wrote, which was 'smaller than I had been told'. Told by whom? The information could only have come from one of the Dieppe maps.

It stands to reason then, that if Cook had these maps in Australia in 1770 he also had them in New Zealand earlier the same year. So he would have been aware as a result that his 'East Cape' had already been dubbed 'Cap Fremose' by the Portuguese, and that the strait which was eventually to bear his name was known up to that time as the 'Gulf of the Portuguese'. *No wonder* while in the 'Gulf' area he kept asking local Maori whether a ship such as his had been in the vicinity before.

Some Answers

So what kind of answers did Cook receive to his question over a seven year period? Because he did get answers, and they were many and varied.

On Tuesday, 16 January 1770, his very first day in Queen Charlotte Sound, he recorded in his journal a piece of information gathered from local Maori:

> These people declared to us this morning that they never either saw or heard of a ship like ours being upon this coast before: from which it appears they have no tradition among them of Tasman being here for I believe Murderer's Bay the place where he anchored not to be far from this place . . .

Although at first glance these tidings appear rather negative, Professor Beaglehole says by way of explanation that . . .

> . . . although the Maori was tenacious of memory, the Tumatakokiri people, who had occupied that part of the country and had killed Tasman's men, were now themselves on the point of extinction, and the remnant left by tribal war was on the run. The absence of tradition is therefore not surprising . . .

Cook had simply been putting his question to the wrong people. Which means any response received would not have signified, and the question of earlier European ships would still not have been settled. But 21 days later, as the *Endeavour* was about to leave the Sound, again an old Maori came aboard to make his farewells and this time when Cook asked his question the man . . .

> . . . answered in the negative, but said that his ancestors had told him that there came once to this place a small vessel from a distant land called

Olhemaroa wherein were four men that were all killed upon their landing and being asked where this distant land lay he pointed to the north, intimating that it would take up a great many days to go thither. Something of this land was mentioned by the people of the Bay of Islands who said that some of their ancestors had been there. But it is very clear to us that their knowledge of this land is only traditional.

In this same story as recorded in the journal of Joseph Banks we learn that there were . . .

. . . two large vessels much larger than theirs, which some time or other came here and were totally destroyed by the inhabitants and all the people belonging to them killed . . .

He further reports Tupaia, the Tahitian interpreter, as saying that this story was a very old tradition, and Professor Beaglehole suggests that it 'may just possibly be a very garbled version' of Tasman's visit in 1642, and the skirmish which resulted in the death of his four men. Whatever the case, this is the first indication in Cook's journals of some type of earlier maritime visitation from afar.

There would appear to be no other indications though – at least not in documents relating to the first voyage, which terminated with the safe arrival of the *Endeavour* back in England again in July 1771. To discover any more information of the type we seek it will now be necessary to jump forward more than three years, except that the circumstances under which Cook obtained this particular evidence will need to be backgrounded first in order to avoid any confusion.

The Second Voyage

Cook had hardly stepped ashore at the end of his first voyage when plans were formulated for a second expedition of the same epic proportions. He was the natural choice again to command the proposed enterprise and during preparations for it was encouraged to have a continuing input, during the course of which many of his ideas were adopted because of his wide experience in these things. One of the ideas floated concerned an escort ship.

Cook reasoned that sailing alone in the vast tracts of unknown waters likely to be encountered again was fraught with too much peril for one vessel on its own and that two ships sailing together would have a far greater chance of survival. The Admiralty Lords agreed, and a second ship, the *Adventure*, was fitted out and Captain Tobias Furneaux put in charge of it. Cook himself, though, would retain overall command of the expedition, and be the sole decision maker in the lead ship, *Resolution*.

Having two ships was a good idea in theory, but there were dangers. They had only to become separated by fog or darkness and the whole idea would fall apart. And this is exactly what happened. The first separation lasted 99 days. The second was permanent.

On 7 June 1773, the vessels had left Queen Charlotte Sound together and struck out to the east and south of New Zealand, still trying to determine whether the great Southern Continent existed, and finished up this segment of the voyage with a northern, western and then southern sweep of the Pacific, taking in such places as Tahiti, Tonga and the Cooks, before returning to New Zealand once more. But the vessels lost each other almost in sight of Cape Palliser and were never to meet again.

The *Adventure* disappeared on 30 October 1773, and on 3 November, Cook entered Queen Charlotte Sound half hoping to see the lost vessel at the rendezvous point in there, but it was nowhere to be found. On 24 November he left the Sound again, but not before writing a note advising Furneaux of his intentions should the *Adventure* eventually show up. The message was sealed in a bottle and buried beneath a tree, on whose trunk a simple message had been scratched – 'Look underneath'. Just a few days after Cook left, the *Adventure* nosed into the Sound and Furneaux found the message. His ship had been driven north up the east coast of the North Island and for weeks was unable to beat southward again to Queen Charlotte. When he did finally manage, it was too late. Cook was well gone. The great navigator was off yet again on a grid pattern search of the seas out to the east and south of New Zealand for a mythical great land mass which he by now had begun to suspect was just that – mythical. Cook's note in the bottle didn't exactly specify what Furneaux should do next and it is likely at this point the *Adventure*'s captain began entertaining the idea of returning to England. His mind was probably made up for him in this regard just as he was about ready to set sail. Furneaux's own account tells the story best:

> On the 17th of December, having refitted the ship, completed our water and wood and got everything ready for sea, we sent our large cutter with Mr Rowe, a midshipman and the boat's crew, to gather wild greens for the ship's company with orders to return that evening, as I intended to sail next morning, but on the boats not returning the same evening nor the next morning, was under great uneasiness about her, hoisted out the launch and sent her with the second lieutenant manned with the boat's crew and ten marines in search of her, who returned about 7 o'clock the same night with the melancholy news of her being cut off by the Indians in Grass Cove where they found the relics of several and the entrails of five men lying on the beach and in the canoes they found several baskets of human flesh and five odd shoes new, as our people had been served shoes a day or two before; they brought on board several hands, two of which we knew, one belonged to Thomas Hill being marked on the back T.H. another to Mr Rowe who had a wound on his forefinger not quite whole, and the head, which was supposed was the head of my servant by the high forehead he being a Negro, the launch fired on them where they were assembled in great numbers on the top of a hill making all the signs of joy imaginable.

This tragedy, according to Professor Beaglehole, 'was one of those things Cook had always gone to enormous pains to prevent'. It appears not to have been a premeditated act, but rather one which arose in the heat of the moment, and which soon got very much out of hand. When at Queen Charlotte Sound on his third voyage in 1777, Cook at last learned direct from the perpetrators how it had all come about.

When Rowe and the nine men with him arrived at Grass Cove in the *Adventure*'s cutter, Furneaux's negro servant was left alone to guard the small boat while the others went off to do their gathering. Just at that point a Maori approached the boat and seized something, whereupon the negro delivered him a hefty clout by way of a deterrent. The Maori objected vociferously and yelled out to those of his companions handy that he was being 'killed'. Attracted by the disturbance Rowe quickly appeared on the scene and began firing his musket. It was all on in moments. 'Once the savage blood was up,' Cook's biographer wrote, 'general butchery and cannibalism followed easily enough.'

If Furneaux had any doubts about what to do next before this incident took place they were now completely gone. Because almost immediately following the disaster he set a course via Cape Horn for England and arrived there on 14 July 1774.

That Question Again

Meanwhile Cook was by now convinced that there was no such thing as a 'great Southern Continent' and returned to Queen Charlotte Sound on 18 October 1774, for a final provisioning-up before going home at last. Furneaux and the *Adventure* were still very much on his mind but he had absolutely no way of knowing what had become of them. Their possible fate had been a worry to him for a whole year now, and he had no idea at this point they were safely back in England, minus, of course, 10 of their number who had come to grief at Grass Cove. But at Queen Charlotte Sound he found the bottled message had gone and noticed also that several trees which had been standing when he was last there had since been cut down with saws and axes. These things reassured him somewhat because it meant only one thing. The *Adventure* had been and was most likely quite safe.

But small niggling doubts were raised again over the three weeks he was in the Sound. During the latter part of October and the early part of November 1774, he asked his old question – 'Has a ship such as ours . . . etc.? – on a number of occasions and received a variety of answers. The significance of some went right over his head. He didn't know that they had been spawned by guilt.

Cook was really only trying at this stage to gain news of the *Adventure*, and being still unaware of the massacre of the 10 men, wasn't quite prepared for some of the information received. Some of the answers puzzled him and made him uneasy. Some, naturally enough, did refer to the *Adventure*, some to the *Adventure*'s cutter which featured in the massacre, and some, seemingly, to vessels completely unknown to Cook – or to us.

The first of a series of exchanges with Maori in the Sound began on 28 October. Cook wrote:

Since the natives have been with us a report has risen said to come first from them, that a ship had lately been lost, somewhere in the Strait, and all the crew killed by them, when I examined them on this head they not only denied it but seemed wholly ignorant of the matter . . .

The report that had 'risen' was first given to William Wales, the astronomer aboard the *Resolution*. As recorded by Cook it went like this. Apparently a ship

. . . had lately been lost in the Straits, that some of the people got on shore and that the natives stole their clothes etc. for which several were shot: but afterwards when they could fire no longer the natives got the better and killed them with their patupatus and ate them. But that they [Wales' informants] had no hand in the affair, which they said happened at Vanua Aroa near Teerawhitte which is on the other side of the Strait. One man said it was two moons ago; but another contradicted him and counted on his fingers about 20 to 30 days. They described by actions how the ship was beat to pieces by going up and down against the rocks till at last it was all scattered abroad.

Two new elements are introduced in this account. These are (a) a ship which had come to grief 'near Teerawhitte which is on the other side of the Strait', and (b), one which was 'beat to pieces by going up and down against the rocks'. Neither of these things is applicable to the *Adventure*'s cutter, even though the remainder of the account obviously is. Cook continues:

The next day some others told the same story or one nearly to the same purport and pointed over the East Bay, which is on the east side of the Sound for the place where it happened. These stories made me very uneasy about the Adventure and I desired Mr Wales and those on shore to let me know if any of the natives should mention it again or to send them to me for I had not heard anything from them myself. When Mr Wales came on board for dinner, he found the very people on board who had told him the story on shore and pointed them out to me. I enquired about the affair and endeavoured to come at the truth by every method I could think on. All I could get from them was kahore and not only denied every syllable of what they had said when on shore but seemed wholly ignorant of the matter – so that I began to think our people had misunderstood them and that the story referred to some of their own people and boats.

It is simple enough to see in this account that the object of the stories *was* the *Adventure*'s cutter and the massacre of its 10 men. Having initially been indiscreet enough to let details of the affairs slip earlier, the Maori people concerned clammed up completely when interrogated by Cook about it to the point where the great man thought he had misunderstood them. We must remember that on this particular day Cook still didn't know about the Grass Cove massacre and this ignorance caused him to view a lot of what he was told less seriously than would otherwise have been the case.

The next reference of interest appears in Cook's journal on 3 November, and must have caused him a great deal of unease. The entry reads simply:

Mr Pickersgill met with some of the natives who related to him the circumstances of a ship being lost and the people killed; but added with great earnestness that it was not them who did it.

Then, on 6 November, there is an entry of further relevance for us. An old Maori friend of Cook's – one 'Pedero' – came aboard and presented the Captain with a staff, to which gesture Cook reciprocated by in turn presenting the man with 'an old suit of clothes with which he was not a little proud'.

Having got him and another into a communicative mood we began to enquire of them if the Adventure had been there during my absence and they gave us to understand in such a manner as admitted of no doubt, that soon after we were gone, she arrived, that she stayed between ten and twenty days and had been gone ten months. They likewise asserted that neither she or any other ship had been stranded on the coast as had been reported. This assertion and the manner they related to us the coming and going of the Adventure made me easy about her, but did not wholly set aside our doubts of some disaster having happened to some other strangers . . .

Pedero was deceiving Cook. As a resident of the area he would have been thoroughly familiar with all the details concerning the untimely end of the *Adventure*'s 10 men, but nowhere in his discourse did he even hint at such a thing. In failing to mention it he was lying by omission. The deception was further cemented in place during the course of a little demonstration in which Cook must have been an undoubted participant, and which we find recorded for us in the Forster writings:

> We made two pieces of paper, to represent the two ships, and drew the figure of the Sound on a larger piece; then drawing the two ships into the Sound, and out of it again, as often as they had touched at and left it, including our last departure, we stopped a while, and at last proceeded to bring our ship in again; but the natives interrupted us, and taking up the paper which represented the *Adventure* they brought it in to the harbour, and drew it out again, counting on their fingers how many moons she had been gone.

The result of all this activity and talk was that Cook now felt at ease about the *Adventure* itself, but, as he put it, the sum total of information received to date 'did not wholly set aside our doubts of some disaster having happened to some other strangers'. And little wonder that he should harbour such doubts. Especially after all the different tales he had been listening to over the previous eight or nine days, some of which featured details of ships being wrecked on rocks and the crews killed. It is quite likely that some other tales were not recorded in the journal, and that Cook wrote down only those representative of the majority. So that the extent of the doubts he admitted to must have been larger than he let on.

Still in Cook's journal on 6 November 1774, and after having just talked about these doubts, we come across something totally unexpected:

> Besides what has been already related, we have been told that a ship had lately been here and was gone to a place called Terato which is on the North side of the Strait.

In a footnote on this particular journal page (151) Cook has scrawled a note to himself in which he says in part 'I hardly know how . . .' (to explain such a thing). This 'Terato' ship had nothing to do with the *Adventure* and whatever it was which gave rise to such a story puzzled Cook greatly, as it to some extent puzzles us today. Next to the footnote just mentioned he has written the word 'omit', as though not quite sure of the merit of what he had just written. The piece has not been omitted, however, and we are left to draw whatever conclusions we can from the fact.

There was no such place as 'Terato' on the other side of the Strait from Queen Charlotte Sound and one wonders whether Cook wrote this down correctly. Did he mean 'Terato' – a place, or 'te rato' – a direction? Rato is the old Maori western quarter and in saying that the unidentified ship had gone to a place called 'Terato', the Maori people may simply have been saying that it sailed to the west.

It was not to be until 18 March 1775 – exactly 15 months after the event – that Cook eventually learned the truth about the misfortune which befell 10 of the *Adventure*'s crew. On the way home to England he met a Dutch vessel and impatiently sent a boat over to it for news – *any* kind of news – of the past two and a half years or so. As Professor Beaglehole puts it:

> Some of the news he got was startling. The *Adventure* had arrived at the Cape twelve months earlier. Furneaux had lost a boat's crew killed and eaten by the New Zealanders. So the confused story gathered on that last visit to Queen Charlotte Sound, on which the people of the place had fallen so obstinately silent, was in substance true. It is obvious that Cook was shocked. He admired the New Zealanders. He stumbled for a comment. 'I shall make no reflections on this Melancholy affair until I hear more about it. I shall only observe, in favour of these people, that I have found them no wickeder than other Men.' (*The Life of Captain James Cook*, 1974)

As for the other stories Cook picked up at Queen Charlotte Sound – stories which had absolutely nothing to do with the *Adventure* or her cutter – the Professor has some interesting comment:

> More important to Cook, and not to be called an interruption, were his efforts to disentangle the truth about the *Adventure*. His informants concurred that she had returned and departed again, in safety. Then what

was the other tale about a ship stranded on the coast, beaten to pieces on the rocks, her crew killed and eaten, some said on the other side of the strait, some on the other side of the sound? – all of which was vehemently denied. Or a third story about a ship which had 'lately' been here and then crossed the strait? Cook felt uneasy, in the end, about the *Adventure*, but could not dismiss the possibility of disaster to some visitor unknown.' (Ibid.)

Not the Least Doubt

We must now jump ahead in time to 25 February 1777, to find the next entry in Cook's journal relevant to our study. And here we find that he seems to have saved the best till last.

One day, on our enquiring from Taweiharooa how many ships, such as ours, had ever arrived in Queen Charlotte Sound, or in any part of its neighbourhood, he began by giving an account of one absolutely unknown to us. This, he said, had put into a port on the north-west coast of Teerawhitte, but a very few years before I arrived in the Sound in the Endeavour, which the New Zealanders distinguished by calling Tupia's ship. At first I thought he might have been mistaken as to the time and place, and that the ship in question might be either Monsieur Surville's [*Saint Jean Baptiste* in 1769] who is said to have touched on the north-east coast of Eaheinamauwe the same year I was there in the Endeavour, or else Monsieur Marion du Fresne's, who was in the Bay of Islands, on the same coast a few years after; but he assured us he was not mistaken, either as to the time or as to the place of the ship's arrival, and that it was well known to everybody about Queen Charlotte Sound and Teerawhitte. He said that the Captain of her, during his stay here, cohabited with a woman of the country and that she had a son by him still living, and about the age of Kokoa (about 9 or 10) who, though not born then, seemed to be equally well acquainted with the story.

We were also informed by Taweiharooa that this ship first introduced the venereal disease among the New Zealanders. I wish that subsequent visitors from Europe may not have their share of guilt in leaving so dreadful a remembrance of them amongst this unhappy race . . . I regretted very much that we did not hear of this ship while we were in the Sound, as, by means of Omai, we might have full and correct information about her from eyewitnesses. For Taweiharooa's account was only from what he had been told, and therefore liable to many mistakes. I have not the least doubt, however, that his testimony may so far be depended upon as to induce us to believe that a ship really had been to Teerawhitte *prior to my arrival in the Endeavour* [my emphasis], as it corresponds with what I had formerly heard. For in the latter end of 1773, the second time I visited in New Zealand, during my last voyage, when we were continually making enquiries about the Adventure, after our separation, some of the natives informed us of a ship having been in a port on the coast of Teerawhitte. But, at that time, we thought we must have misunderstood them and took no notice of the intelligence.

The arrival of this unknown ship has been marked by the New Zealanders with more cause of remembrance than the unhappy one just mentioned. Taweiharooa told us their country was indebted to her people for the present of an animal which they left behind them. But as he had not seen it for himself, no sort of judgment could be formed from his description of what kind it was.

Without a doubt, this is the most detailed account in the written record of a pre-1769, non-Polynesian mariner ashore in New Zealand. Because of the stature of the person recording the information we have little choice but to acknowledge that when Cook said 'I have not the least doubt that a ship really had been . . . prior to my arrival in the Endeavour,' we have no real grounds for disagreeing with him.

After all, he was there . . . we weren't. And the fact he was so willing to give credence to the story tells us a lot. Nowhere in his journals did he ever claim to be the 'rediscoverer' of New Zealand. Nor did he ever claim to be the first European to set foot on New Zealand soil. These are only later ideas. If Cook was so sure he was the first, he is hardly likely to have given away the honour to someone else – especially in the official journal of the expedition which would later be handed over to the Admiralty.

His oft-repeated question to Maori – 'Have you ever seen or heard of a ship such as ours on this coast before?' – indicates he had good reason to believe he *wasn't* first, and that others had beaten him to it.

In fact, he died believing just that.

11

Sundry Unsolved Mysteries

Associated with New Zealand's distant past are a number of minor mysteries which remain unresolved. Each either points to pre-1769 contact by Maori with a culture from outside the Pacific region, or else is concerned with an object whose presence here cannot be accounted for in the light of current knowledge. Although many attempts have been made over the years to resolve the various matters all such efforts to date have failed. This fact has only served to heighten the interest and intrigue which has attached itself to each one. But this is not to say that a resolution is impossible in a number of cases. With objects such as Te Awhio-rangi and the Mauku figurine, a little publicity might be all that is required to strip the mystery from them and expose them for what they really are.

Te Awhio-rangi

New Zealand has its fair share of mystifying objects from the past and, in every case, precise dating and sourcing of the items has been difficult. The Korotangi, the 'Tamil' bell, the Mauku figurine, the Spanish helmet and shot dredged up from Wellington Harbour – little more is known of these today than when first discovered. Now there is another object to add to the list. Known to Maori as Te Awhio-rangi, its traditional history runs uncannily parallel to that of the Korotangi, and we will look at these comparisons a little later on. First, though, the detail surrounding its rediscovery. Because for seven generations it was lost, but is now found again.

On 10 December 1887, while out gathering fungus, a Maori girl by the name of Tomairangi saw something gleaming inside a hollow pukatea tree, which caused her to take immediate fright. It was unlike anything she had ever seen before, and whether or not it evoked some response in her because of an imperfectly remembered piece of tribal lore, or whether the object before her was the same treasured heirloom as referred to in a number of old songs she had heard as a child, no one can say. Whatever the case she fled the scene in panic and alarm in order to get herself as far away from the offending 'thing' as possible. As she went on her way the whole of nature began to convulse in a most uncharacteristic way. The sky quickly darkened, most of the sun's light was shut out and within minutes a fearful thunderstorm burst over the whole area. Snow began to fall as well – in December! A Maori correspondent of *Te Korimako* newspaper (No. 71, 1888) tells us what happened next:

> One of our old men, named Rangi-whakairi-one, hearing the woman and seeing the storm, at once knew that someone had trespassed on a wahi-tapu, or sacred place. He therefore lifted up his karakia, and the storm ceased. Presently all the people assembled and the old man asked, 'Which of you has been to Te Tieke?' The woman replied, 'Which is Te Tieke?' 'Behind there, near the bend in Wai-one.' Said Tomairangi, 'I have been there, but I did not know it was a wahi-tapu. I saw something there, it was like a god, and great was my fear.'

So what was this 'something' which struck such terror into Tomairangi's heart? What had been hidden in the secret place? Evidence for the existence of the object is strictly anecdotal for the moment because, apparently, no European, or anyone outside the Wanganui district, has ever seen it. A century ago the Reverend T.G. Hammond of Patea secured a sketch of the item from a Maori who had seen it and in Vol. 9 (1900) of the *Journal of the Polynesian Society* we learn that although it had been loosely described as an 'axe', 'it is obvious that it is unlike the ordinary Maori axe in shape and size'. Elsdon Best (*Dominion Museum Bulletin*, No. 4) said of it:

> The material of which the Awhio-rangi is made has not been ascertained; but it would be of much interest to do so, inasmuch as it might tend to throw some light on the question of this implement.

There are few other clues to help us identify the object apart from the fact that it is said to be ruddy or reddish in appearance, is bright and shiny so that 'one's likeness can be seen in it', is 18 inches (45.7 cm) long, and is 'shaped like a European adze'. (Axe?) Another description says that it is made from material which 'looks something like china', and that it is speckled and marked in much the same way as the shining cuckoo bird. Best also added that it was probably 'one of the most intensely tapu items now in possession of the Maori people', and that 'very few men would dare, or be allowed, to touch it'.

After its rediscovery by Tomairangi the local Nga Rauru people of Waitotara went to look at the object for themselves and all immediately recognised it as Te Awhio-rangi, the long-lost treasure of their ancestors. There followed a great wailing and weeping and reciting of karakia to the relic, after which it was removed from its hiding place and taken back to the village. Next morning on 11 December at 5.30 am 300 people of the district came to pay their respects. The object was placed on a post so that all might see it, but as the people approached, the lightning flashed, the thunder rolled and 'a fog descended until it was like night'. It took much chanting by the elders before the elements calmed down again, and after the giving of gifts and a lot of further wailing and crying, old songs were sung in which Te Awhio-rangi featured prominently.

According to Maori mythology Te Awhio-rangi is one of several similar sacred items, but this particular one was used by Tane at the beginning of time to sever apart Rangi-nui (the Sky-father) and Papa-tua-nuku (the Earth-mother) because their close and lingering embrace prevented light from coming in. It was credited with god-like powers although Percy Smith said that this claim was nothing much more than a 'subsequent gloss invented by some of its owners to give additional lustre' to the item. But coming over from Hawaiki in the *Takitimu* canoe did not the priest Tupai use Te Awhio-rangi to chop a path through the stormy Pacific waters? Weren't the seas thus severed and spread abroad as a result? When *Takitimu* later visited the Whanganui River the object was given into the possession of the Nga Rauru tribe of Waitotara. Then, seven generations before Tomairangi found it, Rangi-taupea the custodian of the object hid it away for safekeeping at a place called Tieke. It lay hidden until 1887. When last heard of, it was being preserved with the utmost care by the Nga Rauru people and was hidden away so that only its guardians knew where it was.

At about this stage it's difficult not to draw comparisons between Te

Awhio-rangi and the Korotangi because, on the face of it, both seem to be bedfellows. Both were brought from Hawaiki – Te Awhio-rangi on the *Takitimu* and the Korotangi on the *Tainui*. Both were objects of veneration, both were talismanic, both were invested with god-like powers, both were capable of having evil worked through them, and both inspired fear and terror. Both featured in ancient waiata known around most of the country and both were lost and then found again. In each case a tree featured in the rediscovery and each time the item was greeted with wailing and weeping and the singing of old songs. Both are intensely tapu, and both have resisted all attempts by scholars to find out anything about them. And, lastly, both appear not to have been fashioned by Maori hands but, rather, seem to have emanated from a non-Pacific culture. If the Korotangi eventually proves to be authentic, and if Te Awhio-rangi can be made available for study, it may well prove that both indeed came from the same place – at about the same time – and in the same manner.

So to hasten the day of resolution, a simple plea now to the elders of Nga Rauru. Most New Zealanders have a deep and abiding respect for our past, and this is reflected in the large number of libraries and museums around the country set up to preserve what they can of it. We all enjoy the objects on display. They are tangible links with our distant past and help to give us a sense of national identity. In practical terms they demonstrate to our children what the words 'heritage' and 'culture' really mean, and a society without such institutions is very much the poorer for it.

So would you consider allowing all the people of Aotearoa to enjoy Te Awhio-rangi? One of our principal museums would doubtless be thrilled to give this national treasure pride of place for a time. After which, it could be returned to you.

The Mauku Figurine

If asked to nominate the most puzzling of all New Zealand's ancient relics, most scholars would probably opt for the Korotangi – that enigmatic stone bird carefully carved in a non-Polynesian style and said by Maori to have been brought with them from Hawaiki. Others might prefer the honour to go to Te

Awhio-rangi instead, simply because no European has ever laid eyes on it. But there is another item, also carved in a meticulous non-Polynesian style, again of indeterminate antiquity and source, but which this time is totally unknown to Maori and does not feature anywhere in their tradition and lore at all. It is every bit as puzzling as both the Korotangi and Te Awhio-rangi except that – if it were possible – even more so than both of them put together.

What is known as 'the Mauku Figurine' had the experts bluffed when first found at Mauku, near Auckland, in the early years of the 20th century, and has since acquired a further dimension of intrigue simply because it seems to have vanished into thin air. Te Papa Tongarewa has a photograph of it, Elsdon Best wrote a one-page article on it in 1919 but apart from that there appears to be nothing else to show that it ever existed. The principal museums of the country don't know where it is, and one or two have never even heard of it. So it really is a teaser. Elsdon Best's description of the diminutive relic was:

> This object is 2⅜ inches (61 mm) in height and 1⅜ inches (35 mm) wide at its broadest part: material, a soft, friable soapstone. The figure seems to be in a sitting position. There is no hole for suspension. It is no rude Nampa image, but a carefully executed work though having the grotesque aspect so common in Oriental designs. Some form of turban-like head-dress is depicted, also a loose cloak or wide-sleeved garment. The round face shows a wide, short nose. The hands clasp some long object of cylindrical form, the upper end of which seems to show something protruding, and this object bears two transverse serrated designs. The head-dress shows a wide pendant flap at the back. Altogether this snub-nosed Tartar-looking figure represents an interesting discovery when the conditions of that discovery are noted. (*New Zealand Journal of Science and Technology*, Vol. 2, 1919)

And the conditions of that discovery are that the figurine was found imbedded in stiff clay at the bottom of a worn, rut-like track deepened by stormwater and the feet of many cattle. It was face downwards, and its back was flush with the surface. The soapstone of which the figurine is made is very soft and as a result of a cattle beast standing on it a piece has been broken off the lower portion.

The two major problems posed by the find are: had the item been recently dropped? Or had rain and the feet of cattle eroded the track down to where the object had lain for centuries? There can be no clear-cut answers. If it had been recently dropped, it would have had to be *very* recently; perhaps even the day of discovery – or the evening before. Because if a second beast had trodden squarely upon it the figurine would not have survived. Elsdon Best said that because the item was composed of such soft material 'it is clear that it could not be trampled down [any further] into the stiff clay sub-soil by any heavy-bodied creature' (without shattering into small pieces).

Several factors seem to work together to suggest that the relic was already in place long before the cattle came anyway. For a start, it was found in an area connecting two pre-European pa sites whose inhabitants could easily have obtained the item from a seized or wrecked ship in much the same way as the 'Tamil' bell is sometimes alleged to have been obtained. Mauku is not too far distant from Ruapuke Beach – the final resting place of more than one ancient and unidentified vessel. The immediate countryside around the site of the find had only been used by Europeans for 20 years, and only then to graze animals. Also, the design of the object is such that it almost defies identification, which tends to speak of great antiquity in much the same way as the Korotangi and Te Awhio-rangi speak of antiquity. Best talks of a 'tartar-looking' figure which showed a similarity to Oriental designs. However, a work he consulted on the clay figurines of China contained no illustration even resembling it.

To the casual observer the relic has a certain pre-Christian-era and/or Mediterranean or Middle Eastern look about it, but the only way to be sure of anything like this is through intensive research. To date, though, little or nothing has been done and even if the major institutions of the world were canvassed with a photograph – until someone recognised it for what it really is – that would at least be a start. Until such time, it might be better to reserve judgment on this most puzzling little piece of carved steatite. A final word. If anyone reading this happens to know where it is, perhaps they could use their good offices to have it donated into the care of Te Papa Tongarewa.

Even a loan of the item so that researchers could have access to it would be appreciated. Thanks.

Binot Paulmier de Gonneville

The question of whether this French navigator reached New Zealand in 1504, and stayed here for six months, is one which has exercised the imagination of writers for more than 300 years now. Officially, doubt has been expressed about the proposition because the time lapse between the 'supposed event' and publication of it 'is suspicious', and even if there were some basis in truth this interval could have allowed possible 'embroidery to creep into the narrative'. Yet despite this kind of objection no one has really been able to demonstrate that de Gonneville *didn't* come to New Zealand and, until such time as someone does, the possibility remains that a Frenchman was the first European to set foot on New Zealand soil.

Early commentators on New Zealand history were virtually unanimous in proclaiming that there was such a French visit and Dr A.S. Thomson in the 1850s, for instance, said that 'the manner and customs of the islanders where de Gonneville anchored, according to the description given, correspond wonderfully with the habits of the New Zealanders'. But more modern commentators don't seem to share the same enthusiasm. Professor John Dunmore says that although details of the story constitute a 'most circumstantial and tantalising account', and that 'it was reported in more sober terms than were most journeys in the Middle Ages, with just enough information to make it credible', there was not enough to make it verifiable. And so the matter remains largely unresolved to this day.

The circumstances of the story are that on 24 June 1503, de Gonneville left Honfleur in Normandy in command of the ship *Espoir* and a crew of 60 men. Bound for the East Indies, the expedition was funded by local merchants who were no doubt hoping for a rich return from some far-off island there. At first all went well. The ship reached the Canaries in July, crossed the equator in September and, in November, believing themselves to be in the vicinity of the Cape of Good Hope, suddenly found themselves at the centre of a savage storm and were blown off course. That is about where the controversial element in the de Gonneville saga begins because no one is sure what happened next. It isn't clear first of all whether the ship was driven east around the Cape and on into the Southern Indian Ocean, or west into the South

Atlantic and on towards South America. Whatever the case, less than two months later a reasonably large land was reached where the *Espoir* anchored in a river 'about the size of the Orne near Caen'. The inhabitants of the unidentified land treated the French with civility, and the climate and appearance of the place reminded de Gonneville of his native Normandy. He stayed six months repairing his ship and laying in stores for the return journey and when he did leave, took two natives of the country with him: one 'Essomeric', son of a local chief, and another – 'Namoa' – who seems to have been Essomeric's friend, or slave.

Three months into the homeward journey they reached another unidentified land where local trade goods were obtained for the expedition's backers – indicating, according to John Dunmore, that the recently vacated, so-called 'Gonneville Land' was unable to provide such merchandise. Seven more months later, and almost in sight of her home port, the *Espoir* was attacked at sea by the British and lost, together with all her cargo and the ship's papers – such as they were. De Gonneville came through the experience and wasted no time in providing a written account of the epic voyage for the French naval authorities, but he failed to record any co-ordinates for the benign land which had hosted him during the summer and autumn of 1504 and, as a result, spawned a guessing game which has since placed Gonneville Land in a dozen different locations all over the Southern Hemisphere.

Having survived the wreck of their ship, de Gonneville and Essomeric then began to pick up the threads of normal life back in France. Essomeric married one of de Gonneville's relatives and the whole saga slowly slipped into oblivion, and was all but forgotten about for the next century and a half.

Then it was that a descendant of Essomeric's – Jean Paulmier de Courtonne – became consumed by the idea of a return journey to the land from whence his ancestor had come, and the matter of de Gonneville's 1503–1505 voyage, and the land where he had sojourned for six months, were once again brought to public attention. Nothing came of de Courtonne's ambitions but the clamour momentarily raised by him did cement in place in the mind of French merchants and seafarers the notion that somewhere in the southern seas lay a fabulous land which they might be able to exploit, and possibly also lay claim to by right of prior discovery. There is no telling how many French expeditions set out for this part of the world with Gonneville Land as the real magnet. That is, until Cook dispelled the idea of a great Southern Continent with his patient toing and froing in the South Pacific in the 1770s. After that, New Zealand and de Gonneville's utopia came to be linked together more and more.

So what are we to make of these facts? Did de Gonneville reach New Zealand in 1504, or didn't he? Were Essomeric and Namoa Polynesians, or weren't they? Presents received by the ship's company, and which could have identified the mystery country, were all lost in the English attack. Also, parts of de Gonneville's statement seem to rule out New Zealand as being Gonneville Land.

On page 97 of the book *Relation authentique du voyage du Capitaine de Gonneville es nouvelles terres des Indes*, which contains the full text of the Captain's report on the voyage made after his return to France (with an introduction by M. D'Avezac, 1869), we find what seems to be a description of the land and its inhabitants.

De Gonneville talks about 'force bestes', and people whose cooking pots were made of wood covered with clay. This doesn't sound at all like New Zealand, but such early accounts were often garbled, and riddled with inaccuracies largely as a result of being written quite some time after the event. We can gain some sort of an understanding of this by trying to write a detailed report of how we may have occupied *our* time 12 to 18 months ago. Usually, only the highlights will spring to mind – if at all – and painful or stress-ridden periods will have become eroded around the edges by time, and will be difficult to recall in their entirety. Sometimes we'll get it wrong. Sometimes, another person present at the time under scrutiny may furnish a completely different version of events when it comes to recalling them a year or more down the track. So de Gonneville's thinking may well have been a trifle scrambled by the time he came to write his report also. There probably were many animals and wooden cooking pots in one of the lands visited by the *Espoir*, but not necessarily in Gonneville Land itself.

The only copy of the above book in New Zealand is held at the Alexander

Turnbull Library and is available to those who attend the institution personally. No full-length English version of the work seems to exist. A second book, which appears to contain the only other record of de Gonneville's journey to be had in this country, is Pierre Margry's *Les navigations françaises et la revolution maritime du XIVe au XVIe siecle* (1867). Together, these two volumes would be the key texts in this case. Margry was the historian who rediscovered the 1505 account of de Gonneville's voyage, and although he and D'Avezac do not always agree on the interpretation of the evidence, both conclude that Brazil was probably Gonneville Land. However, a few others seem to disagree with this. La Harpe thought North America, Kerguelen thought Madagascar, Laplace thought the west coast of Africa, while La Borde believed it to have been not far from where New Zealand is situated. And when the written record is closely examined most earlier writers do seem to favour New Zealand by a narrow margin.

Some day, with the aid of computers, it may be possible to reconstruct the correct track taken by the *Espoir* even if there is nothing much else to go on except approximate time spans, and then we will know with reasonable certainty whether or not there was a New Zealand involvement. The other way of resolving the matter of course would be to find the wreck of the *Espoir* near the Channel Islands. If mere, tiki and taiaha are found on board, that would be the end of the matter.

The Muriwai Boomerang

In the *Journal of the Polynesian Society* (Vol. 35, No. 1), H. Hamilton tells us of a curious discovery made at Muriwai Beach on 29 November 1925, by Mr A.W.B. Powell of Auckland. Searching among Maori kitchen middens he found something which really shouldn't have been there. It was an Australian boomerang of the type more commonly found in Queensland, and was just about the last thing the amateur archaeologist expected to find among the ancient layers of sea-shells and fish-bones. The wood from which the weapon was made proved difficult to identify; the only positive thing to be said about it was that it wasn't the normal Australian hardwood. There was a feeling at the time that it could perhaps have been fashioned from some kind of New

Zealand wood, but this was never established with any degree of certainty, and all we are left with today is a series of unanswered questions about the matter. For instance, what were old-time Maori doing with an Australian boomerang in their possession? How did it get from Queensland to Muriwai? And when was it discarded? There is no real way of answering any of these questions satisfactorily. But in 1925 – and since – several suggestions have been put forward which could help:

- Perhaps very soon after Cook's last visit, either in the 1790s, or the first decade of the 19th century, traders from Australia brought the boomerang across and gave it to Maori as part exchange for other goods.

- Perhaps before Cook came, a navigator who had previously called at Australia did the same thing.

- In the case of either of the two suggestions above, and having been shown how to use it, Maori may have gone on to try actually making a boomerang from a softer New Zealand wood and, not being thoroughly conversant with the aerodynamic principles of the weapon, found that their New Zealand-made version didn't function properly so eventually discarded it in the midden.

- The boomerang – or the original form from which it was copied – may have drifted across from Australia with the aid of the eastward-flowing currents. Muriwai is not all that far from Ruapuke Beach, the destination of so much other international flotsam and jetsam over the years.

- The boomerang may have been recovered from the inside of a vessel washed up or wrecked on our shores – either pre- or post-Cook.

Whatever the case, it's probably too late now to obtain more specific dates from the midden layer where the boomerang was found. Measuring the carbon-14 content of bone or charcoal specimens surrounding it may have given a clue, but this material is most likely all gone now.

The Shag Point 'Cargo' Boat

One of the most intriguing pieces of Maori tradition touching on the apparent early intrusion of an outside culture comes from the South Island. It was related to J. Herries Beattie in 1920 by the much-respected rangatira – Teone Taare Tikao. According to Tikao, a vessel by the name of *Arai-te-uru* came to New Zealand at the same time as the *Takitimu* canoe but on arrival was wrecked at Shag Point in the South Island. What set it apart from all previous craft to reach these shores was that it is said to have brought a 'cargo of stuff very like Pakeha things, such as frying pans, saucepans . . . basins, and household utensils of various sorts . . . and the seeds on board included wheat . . .' If it had not come to grief in the surf, Tikao asserted, 'the Maori might have forestalled Pakeha ways in New Zealand by many generations.'

This is a difficult one to fathom. Especially as a miraculous element tacked on to the tail end of it plays havoc with any germ of truth it may contain. Apparently, after *Arai-te-uru* was wrecked, 'her crew was turned to stone after getting safely ashore and wandering about a lot'.

The *Takitimu* is one of those canoes which came to New Zealand about 25 generations ago, and if we take note of Tikao's statement that old-time Maori girls 'would often be wed at the age of 13 or 14' – and presumably, produced offspring soon after – then the date of the arrival of both *Takitimu* and *Arai-te-uru* can be placed closer to the middle of the 16th century rather than the formerly held centre of the 14th century. In other words, the event in our featured story took place at the same time as Europeans were beginning to probe the Pacific with their daring voyages of discovery. And since the carriage of wheat seed and the other alleged items on board the *Arai-te-uru* demands *some kind* of contact with Europeans the trick now is to try determining where this contact may have taken place. But we have problems, because this story of the 'cargo boat' as given is a suspicious one. *Something* unusual occurred 25 generations ago but a clue as to why we may never find out the truth about it is to be found in the *Lyttelton Times* at the time of Tikao's death in June, 1927:

He is gone, and his knowledge of Maori folk lore and of the South Island

Maori's history has all gone with him, for there was certain knowledge which the old members of the race could not impart – according to their laws.

The fact is we may not have been given the full story of the *Arai-te-uru* – if such was indeed its name – and the miraculous element may have been tacked on as a smokescreen to hide the truth. It is entirely possible that this whole story relates to a Rongo-tute-type episode and the real details suppressed either because they would have offended the ear of a European listener, or because the laws of tapu required such a thing – or both.

12

The Skeleton of an Ass

Lieutenant Roux's Discovery

An obscure reference in an obscure early journal seems at first glance to provide yet another indication that James Cook may not have been the first European to set foot on New Zealand soil. But the reference and its implications could be misleading. Scholars appear to have sunk the idea that it contains anything of interest to us and, for many, the riddle of 'the skeleton of an ass' is solved. Yet, even so, a small question mark remains.

The journal in which the reference is found was kept by a Frenchman, M. Le St. Jean Roux, while serving with the rank of Lieutenant aboard the French ship *Le Mascarin* which was under the command of Marion du Fresne. Wealth in the Pacific, and discoveries of new land, were the chief motivating forces behind this particular Gallic entrepreneur's decision to set out from the Isle de France (Mauritius) in 1772. In company with another ship, the *Marquis de Castries*, he arrived off the New Zealand coast on 25 March, opposite Mount Egmont. He then followed the coast north, rounded the top of the country, and eventually made a landfall in the Spirits Bay area where the two vessels lingered about a fortnight reviving their scurvy-decimated crews and topping up depleted reserves of water and firewood.

As was the custom with ships making landfall on these epic voyages of discovery after a long period at sea, officers and crew were encouraged to stretch their legs and scout the immediate countryside for edible plants and wildlife and anything else interesting or unusual. It was on one such walkabout that the object of our attention was discovered. And the resulting journal entry, made on 27 April 1772, is the one which has caused so much confusion. Lieutenant Roux (McNab, Vol. 1, 1914) takes up the story:

In the afternoon several of our company went on shore for a walk . . . we

169

noticed an abandoned village . . . I am not aware whether any quadrupeds are to be found in this country, but we found in this village the skeleton of an ass of the same kind as ours, from which I suspect they apparently do possess some species of cattle.

On the face of it there would seem to be nothing very remarkable about this statement – until it is remembered that up to and including the year 1772 there were not, nor ever had been, asses in New Zealand. Roux's discovery needs to be quickly put into its correct historical context at this point to demonstrate just how dramatic and unusually significant such a find would have been in those days. New Zealand in 1772 was still largely unknown to the outside world despite Cook's visit two years earlier and Roux wasn't to know whether the land harboured large quadrupeds or not. His discovery of the skeleton left him quite naturally to speculate that Maori kept 'cattle' – a word of quite broad definition in the 1700s which could be used to collectively describe almost any group of domesticated four-footed animals. Roux seemed quite certain, though, that his skeleton was that of an ass, 'of the same kind as ours', but there is the possibility of course that it could also have been of a half-grown horse or cow.

Jean Roux comes across as quite an intelligent observer. In fact French specialist Professor John Dunmore speaks of him as 'carefully noting down his observations' in his journal. As an 18th-century officer and gentleman Roux wasn't given to embroidery or dramatics in his writings and when compared with other journal keepers of his day survives the encounter exceptionally well. So if he said he saw the skeleton of an ass it must have been. The problem for us today is: how did such an animal come to be in 1772 New Zealand?

Cook or de Surville?

The only possible explanation for the skeleton's presence is that the animal was brought to this country by some earlier European voyager. But who? Orthodox thinking allows of only two possibilities, either Cook or de Surville, and it is to the journals of these two men we must now turn for further clues.

On the day the skeleton was discovered – 27 April 1772 – Captain James

Cook was in England in the last stages of preparing the *Resolution* for his second voyage of discovery to this part of the world. So unless he dropped off a large animal more than two years previously while passing the area on his first voyage, we will have to rule him out of contention. This soon becomes the only course open to us anyway once a sustained examination of his journals is concluded. There is no evidence anywhere to help us with our dilemma. On the contrary. On his journey up the east coast of Northland in late 1769 and down the west coast on his way to Queen Charlotte Sound, there was minimal contact with Maori – apart from a short sojourn at the Bay of Islands – and few opportunities to trade. On 30 November he wrote:

> I gave a piece of Broad Cloth and distributed a few nails . . . and in the *little trade* we had with them they behaved tolerable well . . . [Emphasis added.]

If he had dropped off a large animal, such as a cow, horse or donkey, he would have mentioned it. He always did on other similar occasions. On his first visit to New Zealand in 1769 his *Endeavour* carried only goats, sheep and pigs, plus a few smaller creatures. And because of this it soon becomes abundantly clear that it wasn't Cook who was responsible for Roux's skeleton.

Apart from Cook, the only other contender, that is, the only other European recognised as having stepped on to New Zealand soil before 1772, was the Frenchman, Jean François Marie de Surville. Perhaps it was he who left the large four-footed animal behind just before sailing away from Northland on 31 December 1769.

De Surville left India bound for the Pacific in March 1769, not intending at first to call in at New Zealand, although he probably knew the possibility was always there should circumstances dictate. The purpose of this particular voyage was never very clear and contemporary reports speak of de Surville as 'sailing towards a mirage'. Whether stories of a new spice or gold-rich land in the Pacific were what drew him on, or whether there were more obscure reasons for the expedition, the fact is that none of these things mattered in the end. Before his rendezvous with death on the far eastern side of the Pacific he was forced to alter course to call in at New Zealand because scurvy was decimating his crew and he desperately needed somewhere suitable to rest up.

His ship, the *St Jean Baptiste*, arrived at Doubtless Bay in Northland on 18 December 1769. It had been a disastrous journey. Sixty of his crew had perished from scurvy and the survivors were all within days of suffering a similar fate. Supplies were low, they were about to be beset by life-threatening storms, the ship was in urgent need of maintenance, there were not enough fit men to carry out even the most basic chores and a journal kept by Monsieur Pierre Monneron made the following illuminating comment about the state of the ship and its company: ' . . . a few more days without landing and the vessel *St Jean Baptiste* would never have left New Zealand coasts except by a miracle . . .' Things were *that* bad.

Those of the ship's complement who remained alive were revived somewhat by the fresh food and water at Doubtless Bay during their two weeks' sojourn there but it was only a temporary respite. The decision was taken to run clean across the Pacific to Peru where it was felt facilities for repairing the ship and stocking up with fresh provisions were much more favourable. So on 31 December 1769, with time running out for them, the vessel and its sorry remnant of a crew set off, only to suffer further disaster upon reaching the South American continent.

But did these people leave a large animal behind at Doubtless Bay? That's the question we need to focus on here. We find the answer in the journal of Pottier de L'Horme, first Lieutenant on board the *St Jean Baptiste*.

> We also gave them [Maori] two young pigs, male and female, a hen and a rooster, the only ones we had left . . . *that was all that was possible to part with* in the penury in which we found ourselves. [Emphasis added.]

He couldn't have made it any plainer, and this statement is fairly convincing proof that de Surville was not responsible for Roux's skeleton either. So who was? Which of the nations of Europe had their mariners carrying asses or donkeys on voyages of exploration in the 18th century? The Director of the Nederlands Scheepvaart Museum says that so far as early Dutch explorers were concerned 'donkeys were quite rare aboard a ship, but it is not impossible that a captain may have decided to take one along.' On the other hand, the Director of the Musée de la Marine in Paris is not quite so sure. He says that French explorers of the period did carry cows, pigs, sheep and poultry, but since these creatures were more than enough to congest the rather tiny ships of the period he didn't think the cartage of donkeys would have served any worthwhile purpose. If a beast of burden was required for any particular reason a bull or cow could just as easily have been pressed into service. Some early Spanish ships did carry horses, as did a few English vessels, but there doesn't seem to be any record of them carrying asses. Which raises yet another question or two . . .

Roux Mistaken?

Was Roux mistaken when he claimed to have found the skeleton of an ass? Could it have been a cow or horse instead? This does seem unlikely in view of his own words that the skeleton was that of an ass 'of the same kind as ours' – as though he had been reasonably familiar with the animals back home in France. But we have to look at all the possibilities.

Captain François Bellec of France's Musée de la Marine thinks the quadruped in question may have been a pig or a sheep. He says Roux may not have been talking about an ass at all while making his journal entry and that the whole passage could indeed be a mistake on someone's part, the animal skeleton referred to possibly even belonging to some other unidentified creature.

New Zealand authorities once suggested that Roux may have made a mistake in identifying the skeleton 'simply because of his own ethnocentrism'. He may only have seen the skeleton of a large dog – although the origin of such an animal poses just as much of a problem as the origin of an ass. The somewhat irrelevant question has also been posed by some: 'Did Roux later report actually seeing any such animals living?' For the record, he didn't, and it's difficult to see the point of such a line of enquiry anyway. Because to speak of cows, pigs, sheep and dogs and ethnocentrism as possible explanations for Roux's skeleton is to question the integrity and intelligence of the man himself. Roux didn't leave a large amount of written material behind but, from what he did, it is not difficult to gain an impression of a person who was level-headed, responsible and reliable. He was the kind of person who could easily tell the difference between a dog and a donkey, and it really is worth repeating once more: if he said he saw the skeleton of an ass then we are doing him a disservice by trying to maintain that his discovery was anything less.

A Spectacular Mistranslation

Shifting this enquiry now into a different dimension, the time has come to explore some of the more basic elements of this puzzle. We have established the fact that a responsible French naval officer discovered the skeleton of an ass in Northland in 1772 when such a thing was not supposed to have been possible. We have determined also that such a find raises awkward questions about the early historical beginnings of our nation. The point we must now pursue is whether any mistakes have been made with either language or translation somewhere along the line. This would more than likely have the potential of throwing new light on the matter if it should turn out to be the case. For many decades – in fact since 1914 – scholars have relied upon the original English translation of Roux's passage concerning the skeleton in Robert McNab's *Historical Records of New Zealand*, Vol. 2, p. 365. (Charles Wilson, Chief Librarian of the General Assembly Library at that time, prepared the translation.) According to McNab, Roux originally wrote the following words in his journal on 27 April 1772:

> 'Je ne sais s'il y a des quadrupèdes en ce pays, mais nous trouvâmes dans ce village la forme d'une auge faite comme les nôtres . . .

Mr Wilson's rendition of this passage runs like this:

> I am not aware whether any quadrupeds are to be found in this country, but we found in this village a skeleton of an ass of the same kind as ours . . .

Almost immediately, it will be seen that something is wrong here. One of those involved has perpetrated some kind of basic error because 'la forme d'une auge' does not translate into 'the skeleton of an ass', as anyone with only a nodding acquaintance with the French language will testify. So what appears to be going on? In an effort to find some sort of explanation for this new dilemma expert opinion was sought from appropriate authorities and, as expected, progress was swift. It was discovered that, while the problem of Roux and his skeleton had caused some head scratching in scholarly circles, the mystery had now apparently been solved. Ethnologist Janet Davidson explains:

> This item as translated in McNab's *Historical Records of New Zealand*, Vol. 2, has naturally given rise to a great deal of speculation over the years. However, it seems to be quite simply a spectacular piece of mistranslation from the original French.
>
> The recent authoritative translation by Isabel Ollivier in *Extracts from Journals relating to the visit to New Zealand in May–July 1772 of the French ships* Mascarin *and* Marquis de Castries *under the command of M.J. Marion du Fresne* (published by Alexander Turnbull Library Endowment Trust with Indosuez New Zealand Ltd, 1985) gives us quite a different version.
>
>> We found in this village the form of a trough, made like ours, from which I suspect that they apparently had some sort of livestock.
>
> The Maori did, of course, make quite large wooden troughs for bird snaring, and also had a variety of wooden bowls and containers, some of which are not unlike troughs. This translation makes far more sense, and it is hard to see how the original mistake came about; even my small French dictionary gives 'trough, pig-trough, drinking-trough' for 'auge', and 'faite comme les nôtres' strongly suggests something made by human hand. I am therefore quite satisfied that there was no skeleton of an ass at Spirits Bay in 1772.

We must accept Isabel Ollivier's authoritative translation, and Janet Davidson's endorsement of it, but nagging little questions remain – chief of which concerns librarian Charles Wilson's 1914 translation. How could this very learned man have made such a monumental error in translating Roux's 'la forme d'une auge' into 'the skeleton of an ass' when he made such a seemingly competent and error-free job of translating the rest of the journal? It is extremely difficult to believe he was capable of such a basic mistake.

Senior Lecturer in French at Victoria University, Christiane Mortellier, could find no explanation for Wilson's 'fantastic mistake', but felt that the reference to a quadruped earlier in Roux's passage could have led him to the

Extract taken directly from Lt. Roux's journal for April 1772. In his own neat script the words 'la forme d'une auge' are written so distinctly that the confusion surrounding them can only be attributed to later translators and researchers. (COURTESY OF DES ARCHIVES DE FRANCE, PARIS)

error. She rightly points out also that the only way to make sure of matters of this type would be to get hold of a copy of Roux's original handwritten manuscript and compare it throughout with Wilson's translation as it appears in McNab. Robert McNab himself states (Vol. 1, p. 348) that he extracted Roux's journal account from the records of the Hydrographical Service of the French navy in Paris, and that the Keeper of the Records there had certified it as correct – which doesn't necessarily mean of course that the copying process was entirely error-free. One wonders whether, in the days before portable tape recorders, hand-held cameras and floppy disks, McNab spent long hours sometime before 1914 in France laboriously copying details from Roux's journal into his own notebooks. Because, if he did, it then becomes easier to appreciate how that after many a long hour at such a task it would be natural enough for a mistake or two to creep in – and then to be subsequently overlooked.

Wilson would have been labouring under similar difficulties. Word by word, line by line, transposing from one source of handwritten material into his own. Whatever the cause, a mistake did creep in during the copying and translating process but has now been rectified. There was no skeleton of an ass in Northland in 1772.

13

Mauri, Maui and Maori

A Pre-Maori White Culture
in New Zealand?

In a speculative book of this nature it seems fitting somehow to finish up with the ultimate in speculation about New Zealand's pre-1769 past – that rather than being Polynesian, the first inhabitants of this country were white, or Caucasian/Aryan. It's an intriguing prospect to explore and we'll come to it step by step in the following pages.

The inspiration for the idea of a pre-Maori white culture comes firstly from Maori themselves. They recognised in tradition an ancient race known as 'Turehu', whom Williams defines as a 'supposed light-skinned race who came early to New Zealand' (*Dictionary of the Maori Language*). Until the last decade or two little was known of these people apart from a few vague references in tradition which sometimes spoke of them as having 'copper-coloured' skin, or of being 'ghostly', or even 'fairy-like' in appearance. All of which is traditional Maori nomenclature to describe Caucasians. But some 20th-century theorists have now built on this idea. They are convinced that Maori tradition is correct, and that there were Caucasians in New Zealand long before Maori arrived.

Now in order to advance this idea any further it would normally be necessary at this point to enter the debate over 'the whence of the Maori'. But this is old ground, thrashed out over the years by professional and amateur alike, by the competent and the incompetent, and by anyone else seeking to read into the subject anything they needed or desired to. So we'll steer clear of it. We don't really want to add to the growing dossier of pakeha-generated myths about Maori origins. M.P.K. Sorrenson's book *Maori Origins and Migrations* (1990) with its telling sub-title, *The Genesis of Some Pakeha Myths and Legends*, is enough to deter anyone from such activity.

However, it may be necessary in the following pages to refer to the subject occasionally to allow a better flow of the material.

The debate on Maori origins continues to this day, and there doesn't appear to be any clear-cut resolution in sight. From time to time over the years one proposal after another has gained acceptance only to be supplanted later by what newcomers to the arena considered to be more logical and sound explanations. And it goes on yet.

So in the light of this situation the claim could be made that one theory is as good as another until ultimate light comes along, and that to take a particular theory in isolation, and look at it more closely, can neither be considered a good or a bad thing. As it happens, such an exercise will probably turn out to be a very interesting thing. So let's get on with it.

In 1975 Dr Barry Fell released details of research he had been involved with over the previous 12 years or so – which included an eight-year programme at Harvard University – and came up with some startling conclusions (*New Zealand Listener*, 22 February 1975). In essence the work led Fell to believe that the Maui of Maori tradition was not a Polynesian at all, but rather a brilliant Mauri mathematician and explorer who in a six-ship convoy left Alexandria in Egypt in 239 BC as part of a massive Greek-inspired expedition. Its express purpose was to 'circumnavigate the world, chart the southern skies, and to find gold'. A man called 'Rata' was commander of the fleet and after sailing eastward across the Pacific and striking the American continent he and Maui saw it as an impenetrable barrier so decided to explore the vast ocean they found themselves in instead. Maui then 'pulled up islands wherever he went', to quote from old Polynesian traditions, and eventually finished up in the South Island of New Zealand. From there it didn't take him long to 'fish up' – or discover – the North Island where for some reason he and his estimated 700-strong, light-skinned party settled. Small numbers of Polynesians from an area north and north-west of the country later arrived from time to time and were assimilated by the Turehu pioneers who kept the events alive for us in their traditions.

And where did Fell get all this information? He 'read' about it. Firstly, by deciphering scripts found on old Libyan tombs and stone tablets, and, secondly, by doing the same thing with a wealth of inscriptions present on the Sosorra Cavern walls in West Iran, and which are said to be signed by Maui's own hand.

All startling stuff. And all still hotly debated by the academic community. In fact, a number of scholars have already dismissed Fell's ideas completely; one even going so far as to label them 'hogwash'. But that seems a little harsh in the absence of ultimate truth and doesn't really deter us from pursuing the matter in this chapter – for three reasons. First, Fell has non-Polynesians in New Zealand well before Cook, thus tying in with the principal theme of this book. Second, his account of Maori origins links modern Maori directly with the great classic civilizations of the past. And, third, if only a part of this is true, we will see later on how that in the near future there could be profound sociological and technological implications for New Zealand as a result.

But for us to even consider Fells' proposals we have to be satisfied that such a thing was not only possible more than 2000 years ago in the light of knowledge then prevailing, but that it is also in accord with Maori tradition as well. We will need to be comfortable with such ideas as people living in New Zealand around 230 BC, Maui being a real flesh-and-blood person, the Mauri race being a genuine one, whether or not it was technically possible to mount ambitious long-distance expeditions by sea all that time ago, and so on. We'll take a look at some of these things now.

The First Inhabitants

In 1870, Julius von Haast proposed a scenario which featured 'autocthones' in New Zealand – a race of people so remote from our own time that they roamed the land when 'Cook Straits did not exist', and when 'both islands formed part of a larger island, or even a continent'. They also had 'Melanesian affinities', he said. In playing down this idea, later scholars asserted that von Haast had based his conclusions on a mistaken interpretation of the nature and placement of material found at a moa-hunter campsite, and therefore couldn't be taken too seriously. Yet some theories die hard, and von Haast's old 'Melanesian' and 'palaeolithic' ideas persist to this day in some quarters.

It was Dr Roger Duff in the 1940s who threw most light on this aspect of

Sir Julius von Haast in the 1870s. He suggested there were autocthones in New Zealand – a race of people so remote from our own time that they roamed the land before Cook Strait existed. (COURTESY OF AUCKLAND CITY LIBRARIES)

our country's early beginnings. On the strength of artefacts found at an ancient moa-hunter encampment at the mouth of the Wairau River in Marlborough he was able to demonstrate that what appeared to be the original inhabitants of New Zealand were not only of Polynesian extraction but that their original arrival on these islands occurred far more recently than von Haast had hypothesised. Duff put the age of the Wairau site at about AD 1200 and confidently advanced the theory that the occupants were the direct descendants of the first pioneers who, he suggested, arrived about AD 950 –

at about the same time some Maori traditions speak of Kupe stumbling upon these isles. Artefacts also indicated that the Wairau people were neolithic by classification rather than palaeolithic; that is, their technically advanced polished stone implements were one rung higher up the evolutionary ladder than the crude, earlier chipped stone tools so characteristic of the palaeolithic era, or 'Old Stone Age'.

The date of humans' first arrival in New Zealand was thus set at AD 950 and the people themselves classified as Polynesian. But 16 years after these findings were published Professor Kenneth Cumberland wrote a small book entitled *The Moa Hunter* (1965) in which he began pushing back the dates again:

> By AD 950 the foundations of their [the first inhabitants'] economy were already laid. To have reached such numbers, to have explored a hostile land and to have sought out its resources must have taken some hundreds of years. We can thus say with reasonable safety that the first men arrived . . . in New Zealand . . . not later than AD 750.

Later in the same book he suggests even earlier dates. After discussing hypothetical total population numbers in New Zealand on various arbitrarily selected dates 700 years ago and more he concludes by conceding on p. 10:

> Or we can set back to AD 500 (or even AD 300) the date of the first successful arrival of man.

Of course this would totally sink the idea of a Kupe-led discovery of this country.

Not content with even the AD 300 date, though, Cumberland then left the whole matter wide open with a comment of most refreshing candour:

> Let's admit it, no one knows when men first reached the islands we call today New Zealand.

Later academics have tended to agree with this. In the *New Zealand Journal of Archaeology* (Vol. 10, 1988), N.J. Enright and N.M. Osborne said:

We do not dispute that Polynesian arrival in New Zealand may substantially pre-date the oldest known archaeological sites.

So, therefore, the idea of a human presence in these islands in 230 BC is not at all outside the bounds of possibility. Maui the Mauri circumnavigator could well have been here with his six ships and 700-strong party at that particular time as stated.

Maori tradition is divided on the question of humans in New Zealand prior to Kupe's visit in AD 950, but more than enough exists to support the notion. As Herries Beattie was told, no one particular Maori school of learning had the full story on this subject, or on Maui, and anyone wanting it all would need to canvas every source. Peter Buck said that 'most traditions, though they vary in details, award the honour of the discovery of New Zealand to Kupe'. And it's interesting to see him use the word 'most' in this quotation. It implies correctly that other traditions suggest a different discoverer of New Zealand. Buck's chief source for his information seems to have been the Te Matorohanga school who maintained that when Kupe arrived in AD 950 all he saw here was 'a weka whistling in the gullies, a kokako tolling on the ridges and a fantail flitting about before his face'. In other words, there were no people. But Peter Buck admits in this respect that it is possible that in some parts of the country there were people whom Kupe did not see.

The Aoterangi school on the other hand tells a completely different story. According to this source, when Kupe arrived he found no less than six different 'races' or tribes in residence and learnt from these people that they were 'the descendants of Maui'. Tikao was taught by his tohunga that, way before Kupe's time, a race known as 'Hawea', who spoke a different language to the Maori, and who were 'very dark people with thick mops of curly hair', were the first inhabitants of the South Island, but upon later reflection he remembered being told that even the Hawea found inhabitants already established. And so it goes on, right around the country: some traditions quietly denying the existence of people in New Zealand prior to AD 950 and some emphatically claiming otherwise.

Maui: Man or Demi-god?

Several decades ago, some pakeha scholars were still reluctant to see Maui as anything other than a mythical figment of a primitive imagination. Roger Duff wrote in 1960:

> As Maui was a demi-god, rather than a man, belonging to the folklore of all Polynesian groups, we need not regard him as a literal discoverer of New Zealand.

However, others were not so sure.

Tikao was puzzled by the fact that two totally different versions of Maui's death had been handed down to him: the one advocating that he met his demise in a 'wave heaped high' (i.e. at sea), and the other insisting that he was smothered by the Great Lady of the Darkness – Hine-nui-o-te-po – in a contest which he lost. To add to the confusion is the multiplicity of Maui names. Tikao considered the correct one to be 'Maui-tikitiki-o-te-Raki', or else 'Maui-pae'. Peter Buck has suggested 'Maui-tikitiki-a-Taranga' as being most correct. John White gives other names and a cursory look through the literature reveals yet more, some of which though may only apply to members of Maui's family. It is probably not to be wondered at that after the passage of more than 20 centuries of recording exclusively by oral means that some confusion should be evident, but when we shake it all down we are left with only one reasonable conclusion – that there was more than one Maui. S. Percy Smith advocated this by saying that there were two completely different Mauis, Maui the Demi-god and Maui the Navigator, each divided by an immense gulf of time. Peter Buck was inclined to agree. 'It is probable,' he said, 'that Maui was an early navigator and explorer who lived so far back that he formed a link between the supernatural and the natural, between the gods and man.'

So is there any hint in tradition that Maui may have been fair-skinned? Not directly. Although we are told that Maui's mother was known as 'Tara-ma-i-aia', which John White tells us means '*The Light One* Driven Away'.

By way of a footnote A.K. Newman said of Maori generally:

I am quite convinced they are a hybrid race, dominantly Caucasian, but with a strain of Mongolic blood that is far too large to be ignored . . . The Aryan is the superior strain, for from that came their quickness of intellect. (*Who are the Maoris?* 1912)

The Original Hawaiki Homeland

Over the years many writers have nominated a particular country or area as being the original Hawaiki homeland of the Maori race. Newman, Fornander, Tregear, Smith, Heyerdahl – suggesting areas as far apart as India to South America – have each had their various proposals debated at length, and have each put forward what they believe to be the correct ultimate source of the race.

Ancient Maori tradition – most of it probably Turehu-inspired – tells us what the homeland was like. Maori historian Teone Tikao told Herries Beattie:

> In the beginning, the earth was in one piece, one big land in which lay our ancestral home. 'Kai a Hawaiki' refers to the land coming up when Papa was raised out of the water. Papa was a huge continent, and part of it was Hawaiki, so that Hawaiki as a country dates from the beginning of the world. It was the first country the Maori race lived in, but they have lived in many lands since. (*Tikao Talks*, 1939)

Tikao also said that 'Hui-o-Rangiora was a place near Pikopiko-i-whiti at the end [other side] of the world near where Maui was born.' Maori tradition is quite explicit that the original Hawaiki was a mainland rather than an island. Newman quotes other traditions. 'Iri-hia,' he tells us, 'was a great country from which the original dispersion of the Maori took place. In it was a great temple . . .' He further states that the country was 'great, long and far away, where man – their first ancestor – was created.' In an old tradition quoted by Peter Buck, the country from which the first settlers in New Zealand originally came 'was said to be very hot, and larger than the land to which they came'. Other traditions speak of a very hot original Hawaiki also, one even mentioning the fact that there were large animals there.

The original Hawaiki, then, was far away on the other side of the world, was a huge continent much larger than New Zealand, was very hot, had great temples, and there were large animals present. Such a description easily fits Maui's birthplace – North Africa.

The Mauri Race

Fell tells us that wrapped up in the history of the Mauri race Maori have a whole lost heritage they know nothing about, and that Maui is only the tip of a fascinating iceberg. From inscribed stone tablets discovered in Libya he found details of some of Maui's predecessors who were every bit Maui's equal. Weka is a case in point, and when the sometimes sparse written record is studied Mauri are indeed found to be an extraordinary people – innovative, inventive, extremely talented and endowed with other assorted attributes which are quite unusual. For example, it was from these people we obtained our modern system of numbers, and their alchemy was the baseline from which all modern chemistry has sprung. It would be reasonable to say, in fact, that they are one of history's best-kept secrets.

Mauri originally occupied land where present-day Morocco is situated, although in the third century BC – the time we are most interested in – the country was known to the Mediterranean civilisations of the day as 'Mauretania' – a name not to be confused with the Mauritania of today. This latter application of the word has been described by historians as 'one of the more egregious misnomers of African geography', and doesn't enter into consideration for us here at all.

According to North-West African tradition the beginnings of the Mauri race can be traced to the death of the super-hero Hercules in Spain, and the consequent dispersal of his army there. This force was comprised of a variety of national elements of which the Mede and Persian contingents opted to go south into North Africa after the break-up and settle with the indigenous nomads of the area. The descendants of the Medes became what the Greeks called 'Maurousioi' – later known as 'Mauri', 'Maure', 'Mouri', etc. (which were supposed corruptions of the word 'Mede' – pronounced 'Mai(r)-dai(r)' rather than 'Meed' – while some time later those of the Persians became

Numidians. Yet although both races lived virtually side by side and were subjected to essentially the same influences over the centuries, they began developing in slightly different directions.

Mauri progress accelerated at a much faster rate and the race as a whole soon began to display qualities which set them apart. They became inquisitive as a people, being motivated by a strong desire to expand their horizons, and to acquire knowledge. They quickly urbanised and set up an efficient system of government, although we don't actually hear of a Mauri king until 406 BC. They were attracted to the strongest civilisations around them and, like blotting paper, soaked up new ideas and technology at such a pace that they had to travel further and further afield to find new challenges. Quite simply, other cultures stimulated them. They developed the art of seizing upon the best ideas from these and, in refining them to the ultimate, became a people to be reckoned with.

Together with the neighbouring Numidians they developed a script, and from the Phoenicians they acquired an iron-working technology. The idea of using war-elephants, and chariots, was also quickly taken to heart by them and the stage was reached where Mauri had the reputation of being the best javelin throwers in the whole of North Africa. This of course made them popular with any ruler seeking to build up his army and at one time or another Mauri soldiers fought alongside troops of all the major Mediterranean powers in the last millenium BC. And of course where the soldiers went, Mauri intellectuals and innovators followed.

After Phoenicia, their involvement with ancient Egypt became almost a total-immersion affair. They were attracted like moths to a candle, soaking up ideas, blossoming, and contributing to the old civilisation in ways we can't fully appreciate because of a sparse written record, and the frustrating habit of old Greek historians of referring to all the North African nations (except the Egyptians) as 'Libyans'. There may even have been a Mauri Pharaoh between 950 BC and 730 BC during the period known as the 'Libyan Dynasty'.

Mauri were in Egypt when it was conquered in 325 BC by Alexander the Great who immediately began a widespread Hellenisation of the ancient land. A natural consequence is that Greek culture became the next focal point of

Mauri attention and it is from this particular union that Maui's ambitious expedition resulted.

Several centuries later the mighty Roman empire became the attraction and in AD 700 it was Spain's turn, where, fired up by the message of Islam, they stayed for almost 800 years. Known on this occasion as the 'Moors', they were responsible for an explosion of knowledge generally, and for leaving behind a national frame of mind which allowed Spain in 1492 to send Columbus on a circumnavigation of the earth – a revival of the old Greek/Mauri idea.

Soon after Alexander's conquest of Egypt in 325 BC the city of Alexandria on the Nile Delta was founded to act as the centre of Greek culture. It was there Maui was to meet the great Eratosthenes, the Greek intellectual who computed the circumference of the earth so amazingly accurately that today we can only stand back and marvel at his ingenuity. Maui studied under this man, and Fell says that part of the inscriptions at Sosorra have been deciphered as Maui's concluding steps in calculating the earth's circumference – as learned from Eratosthenes. These inscriptions consist of a few Greek and Egyptian characters as well as the Mauri script, and incorporated with them is a description of an eclipse of the sun which took place at the time of writing. Astronomers at Harvard University have records of every possible eclipse calculated back for 3000 years and this particular one was found to have occurred on 19 November, 232 BC.

Three Greek thinkers – Pythagoras, Aristotle and Eratosthenes – had all suggested that the earth was a sphere but it wasn't until 239 BC that the idea could be put to the test. By then, according to Paul Johnstone (*The Sea-craft of Prehistory*, 1980), the technology was in place to allow round-the-world voyaging to become a possibility because not only had masts and sails been perfected, but keels as a stabilising influence on ships had been introduced, the traditional anchor had been invented, the art of tacking against the wind under sail had been mastered, and, all in all, ships of up to 450 tons burden were commonplace in the Mediterranean area and could carry up to 120 people.

But how did Maui and party propose navigating their way around the world? There were no instruments available to them of the type da Gama and Cook used. There were no maps or charts to speak of either. So was it simply a case of striking off into the unknown and trusting to blind luck? Did they sail by the stars? Most earlier maritime societies had a nodding acquaintance with certain fixed points in the night sky. But these may not have been enough on this particular occasion. Yet what else was available to them? What else could be relied upon to keep them on the latitudinal straight and narrow? The possible answer is both stunning in its simplicity, and near enough to unerring in its accuracy. In all likelihood they would have used nothing much more than a slab of cordierite rock for the purpose, just as the Vikings were suspected of doing 1000 years later when they allegedly reached the east coast of North America by this means. So what is this 'magic' rock? What are the unique qualities it possesses which made it such an indispensable navigational aid to ancient mariners?

Quite simply, cordierite is a mineral which resembles quartz and is distinguished from quartz only with the greatest difficulty. What sets it apart from quartz, however, is the fact that it is pleochroistic. Hurlbut and Klein in their *Manual of Mineralogy* (1993) (after James D. Dana), explain what this means.

> Some minerals show different colours when light is transmitted along different crystallographic directions. This selective absorption known as pleochroism is shown by transparent varieties of cordierite . . .

What this means in practical terms is that the rock has the unusual property of changing colour from blue to yellow depending upon the entry angle of sunlight, and that the reaction still takes place even when the sun is obscured by thick cloud. This feature was known to the Norsemen (c. AD 800 to AD 1000) who used it to establish the sun's position on cloudy days at sea. The story of cordierite as a navigational aid is not very well documented and it is difficult to demonstrate beyond all doubt that Maui and Rata actually did use it on their epic voyage. But there is a small clue which suggests they may have. In the 1920s the learned rangatira Teone Taare Tikao told historian J. Herries Beattie a snippet of ancient lore along the lines that 'it was the god Kahukura who enabled those . . . people to find this land; he sent rainbows . . .' What a graphic way of describing the flash of colour in Maui's hand-held slab of cordierite rock!

So Maui set off from Alexandria in 239 BC as well equipped as was possible for the times. Sailing eastward and hugging the coast, the expedition proceeded via northern India, South-East Asia, New Guinea and beyond to the American continent whereupon steps were retraced, and New Zealand was eventually discovered and settled some time between 232 and 222 BC. Small numbers of Polynesians soon began trickling in from the north of the country and were quickly absorbed by the ever-increasing Mauri population.

But things could have been a lot different. If Maui had succeeded in finding Cape Horn and had been able to return to Alexandria from the west, the history of the peoples of both the Pacific Ocean *and* the American Continent would have been altogether different.

Maori Knowledge of Mauri

After the passage of almost 100 generations does vestigal race memory of Maui's Mauri linger on in modern Maori mind? It does, but only in the most subtle of ways. The word 'mauri' is the most mysterious of all words in the modern Maori language and not too long ago its enunciation was usually accompanied by feelings of fearful reverence. The meanings of the word are incomprehensibly deep and significant, and hauntingly evocative of an immeasurably ancient past. They have to do with the spirit of life, of the well-spring of existence, and what Williams in his dictionary calls 'the life principle, the thymos of man, the source of the spiritual emotions', and so on. A 'mauri' could also be a talisman, a material symbol of the hidden principle protecting vitality, mana, fruitfulness . . . of people's lands, forests, etc.'

But no matter how valiant the attempt, or how competent the person trying, no combination of English words can adequately convey everything the word signifies. In pre-European times the phrase 'tihei mauri ora!' (or, tihi mauri ora!' or just plain 'mauri ora!') had to be forcefully exclaimed before or after certain events to keep the books with the spirit world balanced. Failure to keep faith in this way was believed to invite disaster. When Maori in present times exclaim 'tihei mauri ora!' (or similar), chances are they are not totally aware of the full significance of what they are saying. Perhaps no one can be now. But in so exclaiming, could it be that in spite of themselves they are showing deference to, and paying homage to, their very roots and beginnings? Could, for instance, 'tihei mauri ora!' be broken down as 'We are the Mauri children of Ra'? Or to stretch it out a bit: 'We carry on our shoulders the responsibility of being the great Mauri race of Ra the sun god, and recognising this, and to maintain all the honour implicit in this high position, we must now do or say such-and-such?' – whatever the occasion is demanding at the moment? Ra, of course, is one of the principal deities of the ancient Egyptian spheres of influence to which Mauri were once heavily exposed, and who was wholeheartedly embraced by them.

To act as a focus for things 'mauri', old-time Maori kept revered stones as talismans and marked them with symbols exclusively reserved for the purpose. The use of these good-luck charms was probably begun at the time of Maui; little bits of the old homeland aboard his six ships meeting all sorts of spiritual needs and requirements. And down through the centuries, as the original stones became lost or mislaid, local stones were consecrated for the purpose instead, keeping alive memory of the homeland and symbolising in tangible form the culture left behind. But perhaps of most significance is the fact that in pre-European times Maori referred to each other as 'mauri' on occasion, a use which denoted 'person' in a broad sense, according to Williams, in much the same way as the word 'digger' today broadly refers to an Australian 'person'. And this raises an intriguing question.

Is the word 'Maori' a misnomer? Should it have been 'Mauri' instead? The word 'Maori' to describe native Polynesian New Zealanders did not come into use until about 1850 when Sir George Grey introduced it into his writings. To the pakeha ear there is very little difference between 'mauri', 'mouri', and 'maori', and it is conceivable he could have copied down the wrong one from his informant, and that the name has stuck.

Of significance also is the fact that before Grey began referring to native New Zealanders as 'Maori', other pakeha writers were using a different word.

For instance, in his journal entry for 24 April 1840, while stationed at

Kororareka, Ensign Best says, 'we formed in three divisions but the Mauries (Natives) were not to be seen.' And later: '. . . I went away with a much higher idea of Mauri talent than I had had before.'

In 1841, E.J. Wakefield wrote in his private journal concerning people encountered up the Whanganui River: '. . . they are decidedly the stoutest and best-built mauris that I have seen yet.' And again: '. . . those things which the mauris got by letting the white man live quietly among them.' And once more: '. . . I found mauris and white people much afraid of being attacked by the Taupo tribe . . .'

While Charles Heaphy variously referred to Maori as 'the New Zealanders' or the 'natives' in his writings (*Narrative of a Residence in Various Parts of New Zealand*, 1842), just occasionally he uses the 'mauri' word also. For example, on p. 62 he speaks of 'the discovery of the body of a mauri, who had died suddenly'.

In all cases these pre-Grey writers were using the word 'mauri' in a familiar way as we would use the word 'Maori' today. Is it possible that they were correct, and that we've got it all wrong?

There is another possibility, too. Grey may have copied the word correctly, but totally mistook its meaning as given. The old senses of the word 'maori' were 'usual, ordinary, lesser, and inferior', so that for example a 'rakau maori' was an inferior tree whose timber was not really suitable for anything, 'whetu maori' was one of the lesser, unimportant stars, and so on. Following concentrated settlement by Europeans during the 1840s and 50s many Maori were awestruck by the apparent affluence and technology introduced by the newcomers and went through periods of self-deprecation because of it. This wasn't so much attributable to jealousy, but more to the fact that they saw themselves as not being able to measure up by comparison. Hence the periods of resigned introspection. Grey may have caught his informant in such a mood as this referring to his own people as 'maori' in one of the old senses, and, thinking he had stumbled upon the old-time name of the race promptly wrote it down as such. But he couldn't have got it right. In pre-European times the word 'maori' was never used as a noun. Only 'mauri' was. So there is a very good chance that 'Maori' (with a capital 'M') is a pakeha invention.

A New Mauri Beginning

Maui the mathematician, astronomer, navigator and explorer was probably forced to settle in New Zealand owing to the rundown state of his ships and the lack of facilities and resources to repair them. Cut off from the necessary inspirational proximity of a greater nation for the first time in centuries the fledgling Mauri colony probably had a full-time job surviving, and little opportunity to concern themselves with anything else. As a consequence they would have soon lost the arts of iron-making, pottery, writing and the building of stone structures. Although, the remnants of these things could well be hiding in the depths of some Northland forest yet.

The potential of these people didn't wither and die in those early days; it simply went into a long hibernation from which it is only now beginning to stir. For 2000 years in this country a great pool of explosive Mauri genes has been slumbering away like seeds in a packet – waiting for someone to break the seal, waiting to be watered and nurtured, waiting to come up against a culture that would make them burst forth and blossom again. And now the wait is over.

You have only to study each issue of *Kokiri Paetae* to see this. Described by the Ministry of Maori Development as a 'celebration of Maori achievement', this monthly paper is filled with all sorts of positive news as issue after issue highlights progress by Maori on all fronts. It shows how they are achieving at a rate not known before and, in essence, records the awakening of a people. In some fields of endeavour Maori are beginning to lead out and to show the way and, if this renaissance continues, it won't be long before they are giving new meaning to the words 'innovation' and 'excellence' from one end of the country to the other. May it soon be so.

Conclusion

The belief that Europeans and other non-Polynesians were present in New Zealand before Cook's arrival in 1769 is an integral part of both Maori *and* Pakeha folklore. For generations, the notion has pulsated with a life of its own. And it's not hard to see why. The sheer volume and quality of circumstantial evidence is such that it is difficult to reach any other conclusion about pre-1796 intruders. Admittedly there is a serious lack of hard documentary evidence but that doesn't necessarily mean it doesn't exist, or that the suspected events didn't take place. It simply means that we haven't been looking hard enough. Or we've been looking in the wrong places. There is no documentary evidence for humanoid life forms on distant planets either. But since the balance of probabilities demands such a thing few scientists on Earth would summarily discount the likelihood if pressed. There *must* be people out there somewhere, just as there must have been non-Polynesians in New Zealand before 1769.

There may be simple explanations for some of what is put forward in this book but we are still left with many questions for which no answers are currently possible. Seeing the extent of the material here may hearten those who already believe in a pre-1769, non-Polynesian presence, waverers may have been induced to finally make up their minds about the subject, and as for the hard-bitten dyed-in-the-wool skeptics – at least they will have been given food for thought.

And anything which makes intelligent people think can't be all bad.

Author's Note

The material in this book represents only a fraction of what is available on the subject, and features some of the highlights only. Restrictions on space meant that the sifting process had to be particularly vigorous, but that doesn't mean to say that the information excluded is any less fascinating, or important – because it isn't. Much of it has been held over for inclusion in a planned follow-up volume and there will be space available for any new material which may come forward in the meantime. So if anyone is able to expand on any of the topics herein, or has other information indicating the presence of non-Polynesians in New Zealand before 1769, I would be interested to hear from them. I can be contacted through the publisher.

Bibliography

Alfonse, J. *Voyages Avantureux*, Jan de Marnef, Poitiers, France, 1559.

Bagnall, A.G. *Wairarapa – An Historical Excursion*, Masterton, 1976.

Bagnall, A.G. and Peterson, G.C. *William Colenso*, A.H. and A.W. Reed, Wellington, 1948.

Balantyne-Scott, N. *Trail Blazers of New Zealand*, Duff Syndications, Wellington, 1974.

Bawden, P. *The Years Before Waitangi*, Benton Ross, Auckland, 1987.

Beaglehole, J.C. (ed.) *The Journals of Captain James Cook*, 3 Vols., Cambridge, 1955–74.

Beaglehole, J.C. *The Discovery of New Zealand*, Oxford University Press, London, 1961.

Beaglehole, J.C. *The Life of Captain James Cook*, Hakluyt Society, London, 1974.

Beattie, J.H. *Tikao Talks*, Reed, Wellington, 1939.

Begg, A.C and Begg, N.C. *Port Preservation: The Story of Preservation Inlet and the Solander Grounds*, Whitcombe and Tombs, 1973.

Best, E. *Waikaremoana – The Sea of Rippling Waters*, Government Printer, Wellington, 1897.

Best, E. 'The Finding of Te Awhio-rangi Axe', *Journal of the Polynesian Society*, Vol. 9, 1900.

Best, E. 'Te Awhio-rangi', *Dominion Museum Bulletin*, No. 4, 1912.

Best, E. 'Stone Implements of the Maori', *Dominion Museum Bulletin*, No. 4, 1912.

Best, E. 'The Ship of Rongotute', *Journal of Early Settlers and Historical Association of Wellington*, Vol. 1, No. 1, 1912–1913.

Best, E. 'The Land of Tara and they who Settled it (part iv)', *Journal of the Polynesian Society*, Vol. 28, 1919.

Best, E. *Tuhoe*, Thomas Avery, New Plymouth, 1925.

Best, E. 'The Maori Canoe', *Dominion Museum Bulletin*, No. 7, 1925.

Best, E. 'Maori Agriculture', *Dominion Museum Bulletin*, No. 9, 1925.

Best, E. 'Notes on a Curious Steatite Figurine found at Mauku, Auckland', *Journal of the Polynesian Society*, Vol. 35, 1926.

Best, E. 'Notes on the Korotangi or Stone Bird', *Journal of the Polynesian Society*, Vol. 38, No. 1, 1929.

Biggs, B. et al. *The New Zealand Junior Encyclopaedia*, New Zealand Educational Foundation (Northern) Ltd., Wellington, 1960.

Boissais, E. *Binot Paulmier dit le Capitaine de Gonville, son voyage, sa descendance*, Caen, 1912.

Bréard, C. *Notes sur la Famille du Capitaine Gonneville*, Rouen, 1885.

Buck, P. (Te Rangi Hiroa). *The Coming of the Maori*, Maori Purposes Fund Board, 1949.

Buick, T.L. *Old Marlborough*, Capper Press, Christchurch, 1976.

Buller, Rev. J. *Forty Years in New Zealand*, Hodder & Stoughton, London, 1878.

Byron, K.W. *Lost Treasures in Australia and New Zealand*, Reed, Wellington, 1965.

Cruise, R.A. *Journal of a Ten Months' Residence in New Zealand*, Capper Press, Christchurch, 1974. (Originally published 1823, Longman Hurst, London.)

Cumberland, K. *The Moa Hunter*, Whitcombe and Tombs, 1965.

D'Avezac, M. *Relation authentique du voyage du Capitaine de Gonneville es nouvelles terres des Indes*, Challamel, Paris, 1869.

Davidson, J. *The Prehistory of New Zealand*, Longman Paul, Auckland, 1984.

Dieffenbach, E. *Travels in New Zealand*, 2 Vols., John Murray, London, 1843.

Dominion newspaper, article on the 'Spanish' helmet dredged up from Wellington Harbour c. 1906, 28 February 1924.

Dominion newspaper, article on the supposed similarity between some Spanish and Maori words, 9 February 1926.

Duff, R. *The Moa Hunter Period of Maori Culture*, Wellington, 1950.

Duff, R. 'The Coming of the Maoris', *The New Zealand Junior Encyclopaedia*, Vol. 1, New Zealand Educational Foundation (Northern) Ltd., Wellington, 1960.

Duncan, W. *Memories of an Early Settler*, Morton, 1929.

Elvy, W.J. *Kei Puta te Wairau*, Whitcombe and Tombs, Christchurch, 1957.

Enright, N.J. and Osborne, N.M. 'Early Polynesians in New Zealand', *New Zealand Journal of Archaeology*, Vol. 10, 1988.

Evening Post newspaper, article on the 'Spanish' helmet dredged up from Wellington Harbour c. 1906, 27 June 1953.

Fell, B. 'Maoris from the Mediterranean', *New Zealand Listener*, 22 February 1975.

Fell, B. 'How Ancient Maori Was Written', *New Zealand Listener*, 1 March 1975.

Fell, B. 'An Ancient Maori Text in Libyan Script from Otaki, New Zealand', Epigraphic Society, March 1975.

Gazel, A. *French Navigators and the Early History of New Zealand*, Harry H. Tombs, Wellington, 1946.

Graham. G. 'The Legend of the Korotangi', *Journal of the Polynesian Society*, Vol. 26, 1917.

Grey, G. *Poems, Traditions and Chaunts of the Maoris*, 1853.

Hamilton, H. 'The Muriwai Boomerang', *Journal of the Polynesian Society*, Vol. 35, No. 1, 1926.

Harding, S. 'An examination of the mystery wreck of Ruapuke Beach', Auckland Institute & Museum report, October, 1892.

Heaphy, C. *Narrative of a Residence in Various Parts of New Zealand . . .*, Smith, Elder and Co., Cornhill, 1842.

Hervé, R. *Chance Discovery of Australia and New Zealand by Portuguese and Spanish Navigators between 1521 and 1528*, translated from the French by Prof. John Dunmore, Dunmore Press, Palmerston North, 1983.

Hilder, B. 'The Story of the Tamil Bell', *Journal of the Polynesian Society*, Vol. 84, No. 4, 1975.

Hombron, J.B. *Aventures les plus curieuses des voyagers coup d'oeil autour du monde . . .*, Paris, 1847.

Howard, B. *Rakiura – Stewart Island, New Zealand*, Reed, Wellington, 1974.

Hunt, C.G. 'Some Notes on the Mystery Wreck on Ruapuke Beach for the Waikato Scientific Association', Unpublished manuscript, 1955. (University of Waikato Library.)

Hurlbut, C.S. and Klein, C. *Manual of Mineralogy*, Wiley, New York, 1993.

Ingram, C.W. and Wheatley, P.O. *New Zealand Shipwrecks*, Reed, Wellington, 1961.

Jenkin, R. *New Zealand Mysteries*, Reed, Wellington, 1970.

Johnstone, P. *The Sea-craft of Prehistory*, Routledge and Kegan Paul, London and Henley, 1980.

Jones, P. *Nga Iwi o Tainui*, Auckland University Press, Auckland, 1995.

Kauika, W. Article on Te Awhio-rangi, *Te Korimako* newspaper, No. 71, 1888.

Kelly, L.G. *Marion du Fresne at the Bay of Islands*, Reed, Wellington, 1951.

Keyes, J.W. 'The Ngatimamoe', *Journal of the Polynesian Society*, Vol. 76, No. 1, 1967.

'Kronan – Remnants of a Mighty Warship', *National Geographic*, April, 1989.

Langdon, R. *The Lost Caravel Re-explored*, Brolga Press, Sydney, 1988.

Lee, S. and Kendall, T. *A Grammar and Vocabulary of the Language of New Zealand*, London, 1820.

Legge, C.A. PhD Thesis: 'Dumont d'Urville, J. A transcription of Dumont d'Urville's manuscript "Les Zélandais histoire australienne" and the accompanying notes, followed by a study of some literary and historical aspects of the text', 1989.

Lyttelton Times newspaper, article on death of Teone Tikao, June 1927.

Mackay, C. 'Korotangi – An Enigmatic Stone Bird', *Dominion Museum Records in Ethnology*, Vol. 2, No. 10, 1973.

Maling, P.B. *Early Charts of New Zealand 1542–1857*, Wellington, 1969.

Margry, P. *Les navigations françaises et la revolution maritime du XIVe au XVIe siecle*, Tross, Paris, 1867.

Maskell, W.M. Minutes of a meeting of the Wellington Philosophical Society held 31 July 1889. As recorded in 'Transactions of the New Zealand Institute', Vol. 22.

McConnell, R. *Olive Branches*, privately published, Gisborne, 1980.

McIntyre, K.G. *The Secret Discovery of Australia*, Melindie, South Australia, Souvenir Press, 1977.

McKillop, Lt H.F. *Reminiscences of Twelve Months' Service in New Zealand*, Bentley, London, 1849.

McNab, R. *Murihiku and the Southern Islands*, Smith, London, 1907.

McNab, R. *Historical Records of New Zealand*, 2 Vols., Government Printer, Wellington, 1914.

McNab, R. *The Old Whaling Days*, Golden Press, Auckland, 1975.

Mitcalfe, B. 'Korotangi, the Sacred Bird', *Te Ao Hou*, No. 37, December 1961.

Newman, A.K. *Who are the Maoris?*, Whitcombe and Tombs, Christchurch, 1912.

New Zealand Herald newspaper, 'Conquistadors on the Kaipara', Pat Hanning, 19 May 1990.

Nicholas, J.L. *Narrative of Voyage to New Zealand*, 2 Vols., Black, London, 1817.

Ollivier, I. *Extracts from Journals relating to the visit to New Zealand in May–July 1772 of the French ships* Mascarin *and* Maquis de Castries, Alexander Turnbull Library Endowment Trust with Indosuez New Zealand Ltd., 1985.

Polack, J.S. *New Zealand: Being a Narrative of Travels and Adventures*, 2 Vols., Capper Press, Christchurch, 1974. (Originally published 1838, Bentley, London.)

Pomare, M. *Legends of the Maori*, Vol. 2, H.H. Tombs Ltd., 1934.

Power, W.T. *Sketches in New Zealand*, London, 1849.

Raglan County Chronicle newspaper, article on the mystery shipwreck at Ruapuke Beach, 10 January 1903.

Reedy, A. *Nga Korero o Mahi Ruatapu*, Canterbury University Press, Christchurch, 1993.

Reeves, W.P. *The Long White Cloud*, Horace Marshall & Son, London, 2nd ed., 1899.

Robertson, J. *The Captain Cook Myth Exploded*, Angus and Robertson, Sydney and London, 1981.

Salmond, A. *Two Worlds*, Viking, Auckland, 1991.

Saunders, *A. History of New Zealand 1642–1861*, Whitcombe and Tombs Ltd, Christchurch, 1896.

Sharp, A. *Crisis at Kerikeri*, Reed, Wellington, 1958.

Sharp, A. *The Voyages of Abel Janszoon Tasman*, Oxford University Press, London, 1968.

Sherrin, R.A. and Wallace, J.H. *Early History of New Zealand*, Brett, Auckland, 1890.

Shortland, E. *The Southern Districts of New Zealand*, London, 1851.

Sinclair, K. *A History of New Zealand*, Penguin, Auckland, 1988.

Smith, S.P. 'Wars of the Northern against the Southern Tribes . . .', *Journal of the Polynesian Society*, Vol. 8, 1899.

Smith, S.P. 'Some Whanganui Historical Notes', *Journal of the Polynesian Society*, Vol. 14, 1905.

Sorrenson, M.P.K. *Maori Origins and Migrations*, Auckland University Press, Auckland, 1990.

Stokes, E. 'European Discovery of New Zealand Before 1642', *New Zealand Journal of History*, Vol. 4, No. 1. April 1970. An informative resume of European discovery of New Zealand before 1642 (Tasman).

Taylor, N.M. *Early Travellers in New Zealand*, Oxford University Press, London, 1959.

'The Maori Belief in the Supernatural Powers of Certain Axes', *Journal of the Polynesian Society*, Vol. 28.

Thomson, A.S. *The Story of New Zealand*, Capper Press, Christchurch, 1974 (originally published 1859).

Thomson, G.M. *The Naturalisation of Animals and Plants in New Zealand*, Cambridge University Press, London, 1922.

Transactions of the New Zealand Institute, Vol. 22, pp. 499-508, 522-527, regarding the Korotangi.

Tregear, E. *The Maori Race*, A.D. Willis, Wellington, 1904.

Trolove, F.J. *Ruapuke: the Early Days*, A.O. Rice, 1970.

von Haast, J. 'Researches and excavations carried on in and near the Moa Bone Point Cave . . .', Record of an address given to the Philosophical Institute of Canterbury, Christchurch, 1874.

Wade, W.R. *Journey in the Northern Island of New Zealand*, Capper Press, Christchurch, 1977 (first published 1838).

Watt, R. Notes on the 'Spanish' helmet, National Museum Records.

White, J. *Ancient History of the Maori*, 6 Vols., Government Printer, Wellington, 1888.

Williams, H.W. *A Dictionary of the Maori Language*, Government Printer, Wellington, 1917.

Wright, H.M. *New Zealand 1769–1840*, Harvard University Press, Cambridge, Mass., 1980.

Wright, O. *New Zealand 1826–1827*, Wellington, 1950.